D1333414

THE BRITISH CONSTITUTION

General Editor
LORD STAMP

*CAMBRIDGE
UNIVERSITY PRESS*
LONDON: BENTLEY HOUSE
*NEW YORK, TORONTO, BOMBAY
CALCUTTA, MADRAS: MACMILLAN
TOKYO: MARUZEN COMPANY LTD*

W. IVOR JENNINGS

M.A., LL.D.

Principal of the Ceylon University College;
of Gray's Inn, barrister-at-law

THE BRITISH CONSTITUTION

CAMBRIDGE
AT THE UNIVERSITY PRESS
1941

To

L. S. E.

GENERAL EDITOR'S PREFACE

There were many writers upon the British Constitution before Walter Bagehot, but they were mostly lawyers and detached observers of structure, whereas he, with his daily contacts with Ministers and Government Departments, saw motive and method from within. He was sensitive to the differences between theory and practice, and the regularity with which outmoded practice became newly accepted theory. He gave the subject at once the actuality of the finest journalism and yet brought it for the first time under the scientific discipline of analysis and established causation. He fitted it too to be an item in an academic curriculum. Fortunately for us, he did not wait, like Courtney, to reach his seventies before garnering the fruit of a long experience of government from within, but his forty years of age were ripe with accumulated impressions. Books on this subject then came out at long intervals and each in turn was absorbed as the authority for its decade. To-day they pour from the press, mostly by professional and professorial observers of government from more or less detached angles, most of them excellent in their own field, and each contriving, owing to the greater width and richness of the subject-matter, to present novel aspects and original comment. Bagehot spoke of the main difficulty of his task as involved in the fact that the object "is in constant change, a 'living' thing", which must be seized for a static picture at some point of time. Courtney, also, said the unique characteristic of our constitution is that it is subject to constant and continuous growth and change. "It is a living organism, absorbing new facts and transforming itself." But modern writers do not dwell much on this difficulty of movement—it is taken for granted and circumvented by the issue of books at much more frequent intervals. They do, however, insist more and more on the search for the true dominants of action, and with a kind of political psycho-analysis try to discover the real springs of change.

One need not be surprised that foreigners find this subject baffling. But one of the best informed and most penetrating studies of our constitution that has come from a foreigner also emphasises not so much rapidity of change, as this deceptive appearance of form. Karl Heinz Abshagen—for ten years resident in England, and a correspondent of German newspapers—in his *King, Lords and Gentlemen* (1938), says that "a satisfactory account of the peculiar play of the forces which, behind the façade of parliamentary forms, actually determine the course of British policy, would have to be written by one of the men who are themselves an element in these operative forces". But he suggests that many of the men playing an important part may be actors in either principal or lesser roles without dreaming that they are playing any part at all—"they exercise their power unwittingly and so with a complete lack of self-consciousness". This may be an over-emphasis, but it serves to show the change in the objective. To-day the writer is tempted to disbelieve every outward form and to say "That is only how it is *supposed* to work: this is how it *appears* to work and, therefore, there must be some other way in which it actually *does* work", and he thus aims at a subjective penetration of the whole subject. The reader tends to get into the same frame of mind—in fact, an American friend declared he judged the merits of a book on British Government according to its power to give "the low-down on the high-spots".

Formerly, the difficulty was to extract the permanent from the transient, or to convey a sense of orderly growth in a fixed description. This evidently does not impress Abshagen who, on the contrary, associates our democratic constitution more with the notion of permanence. He says that British democracy is the only Governmental system in Europe that has passed through the tempests of the last forty years with no fundamental modification. It is a reality not so much because of careful observance of democratic forms and parliamentary usage, as because of the great *potential* influence of public opinion in every decision of major importance. And most modern writers, though not thinking of relative permanence, strike the same note. It is the ultimate sovereignty of public opinion which is the keystone to the Constitution.

But how public opinion is formed or developed and which parts of the formal constitution influence it, and how it is made articulate, are subjects of much greater complexity, with room for illustrations of all kinds. Mr Keynes once described (*A Revision of the Treaty* 1922, p. 4) the two opinions of to-day—"not as in former ages, the true and the false, but the outside and the inside". Then he found there were really *two* outside opinions—"that which is expressed in the newspapers and that which the mass of ordinary men privately suspect to be true". It is no part of a study of the British Constitution to develop the social psychology of the formation of opinion. But the parallel development of readiness to act, somewhere inside this machine, is of the heart of the subject. When opinion has been gradually "becoming ripe", who in this complicated constitutional society gets or gives the final shove that puts new policy into the programme? It may be a violent correspondence in *The Times* affects Ministers directly; a pertinacious series of questions in the House; a conversation between Sir Warren Fisher and Sir Horace Wilson deciding to "put it up" to the Chancellor; the report of a Royal Commission; or the word of one of the Prime Minister's personal friends. For each Prime Minister has had his little group of intimates, sometimes hardly known to the public, or officials acting out of school, who have had great influence on the moment and manner of "pulling the trigger", and even on policy itself. The Weirs, Colwyns, Beaverbrooks, Tom Jones's, Wilsons, pass unseen through the pages of power. But the pursuit of these personalia is only the gossip of the subject, and not the subject itself.

Those who know Dr Jennings's *Cabinet Government* know that he can be a worthy representative of the older ideals of solid and permanent description. Here, as he says himself, he is writing about the British Constitution 'primarily in relation to existing conditions'. In thus securing a vivid actuality for his treatment, Dr Jennings would be the first to admit that he is running certain risks. Some of the numerous illustrations from events hot from the oven, concerning which we have no more than journalistic knowledge of causes and intentions, may, in the course of time not far ahead, take on a different complexion as knowledge grows and the background settles. But Dr Jennings's book is not a textbook for examinees; it is a work intended for wider circles, and current assessments of still throbbing events, combined with the constitutional changes they seem to portend, are not only provocative, but, coming from so shrewd and experienced a judge, are provisionally most instructive.

So devastating a social upheaval as this war involves must mean considerable constitutional developments too, and a survey of the latest position as from which they must take place is a public service.

STAMP

PREFACE

The last words of this book were written during an air raid warning, and the drone in the distance indicated the approach of enemy aircraft. The circumstance drew my attention for the first time to the fact that for three months I had continued to write about the British Constitution in complete disregard of almost daily prophecies from over the water that the next week was to see its overthrow. The exercise was no bravado on my part; it was, I suppose, the normal reaction of a constitutional lawyer who has perforce to think in centuries rather than in weeks, and for whom, therefore, immediate threats fall into a historical perspective. He has, so to speak, heard them so often in the past that he unconsciously discounts them in the present. The effects of the war are nevertheless evident in the book. Some of the examples which seemed most convenient were drawn from present experience; sometimes an immediate controversy, such as that over secret sessions, compelled an ancient principle to be more emphatically stated; and it appeared desirable to include a special chapter on war-time government.

The British Constitution is always topical, and no apology is necessary for writing about it primarily in relation to existing conditions. Perhaps, however, an apology is required for writing about it at all. So many good books have been written on the subject in recent years that an addition to their number may appear otiose. My first line of defence is that I was asked to write. My real justification is, however, that for some years I have been conducting a systematic survey of British political institutions. The survey is by no means completed, and if there had been no war I should have refrained from writing a small book until it was. The outbreak of war made it impossible to continue certain studies on which I was engaged, though some tentative conclusions appear in the first two chapters of this book. The rest is founded upon large-scale studies which have already been published by the Cambridge University Press. I have not tried to summarise those books. It appeared to me that the reader would prefer a discussion of problems to a statement of practice, and I hope that, if he needs further information, he will look up the relevant portions of *Cabinet Government* and *Parliament*. Not all the difficulties of the British Constitution have been discussed, because I have kept to those which seemed at once most controversial and most important. Nor have I sought to make a sustained defence of democratic principles and of the liberties upon which they are based, because it did not appear that they required defence. The aim has been to give the ordinary citizen a readable and detached (though not, of course, impartial) introduction to the problems of the governmental system in which he plays so large a part, and at the same time to describe for the benefit of our friends overseas the one remaining democratic system (other than Eire) in western Europe.

On the day on which the manuscript was completed I learned that my connection with the London School of Economics and Political Science was about to be suspended. It is therefore fitting that I should express to my colleagues my gratitude for what I have learned from them during my eleven years' association with the School. Once more, also, I owe a deep obligation to Mr A. D. Hargreaves, of the University of Birmingham, who on this occasion has relieved me of the necessity of seeing the book through the press.

W. I. J.

6 *September* 1940

CONTENTS

ILLUSTRATIONS

CHAPTER I

GOVERNMENT BY THE PEOPLE

§ 1. *We, the People*

In one of the least prudent of his speeches, Joseph Chamberlain used a phrase which has become historic. He was defending proposals made by the Unionist Government but opposed by the Liberals for the making of additional grants to members of the Royal Family. That in itself was enough to anger the Liberals, for Joseph Chamberlain the Unionist was now supporting what Joseph Chamberlain the Radical had opposed in almost republican speeches. Stung by Opposition taunts, he jeered at "honourable members who profess on all occasions to speak for the People with a capital P". He went on to say: "These honourable members tell us it is a shameful thing to fawn upon a monarch. So it is; but it is a more shameful thing to truckle to a multitude." Truckle to a multitude? The Liberal party was not likely to forget that phrase and there must have been hundreds of platforms from which Liberal speakers for the next decade reminded "the People with a capital P" what Joseph Chamberlain thought of them.

In doing so they were falsifying his character. Chamberlain more than any Unionist statesman of the late nineteenth century except perhaps Lord Randolph Churchill recognised the need to bow to public opinion—

to truckle to the multitude. He had come into national politics at the head of a popular movement in Birmingham; he had inspired the "unauthorised programme" of 1884 because he believed that the people wanted something more positive than the Liberal leaders were offering them; later on, he restrained Lord Milner's ardour for war against the Transvaal until he was sure that the larger section of public opinion had been convinced of the inevitability of a conflict; and one of the reasons for his raising the banner of "tariff reform" after 1900 was his belief that the Unionists, who had snatched a majority in the "khaki election", would be heavily defeated next time if they did not capture the electors' imagination. That he proved to be wrong in his choice of remedy does not prove that his diagnosis was faulty.

In this respect Chamberlain was more in tune with the spirit of the Constitution after 1884 than any of the leaders of the Liberal party, not excepting Gladstone. He was far more the democratic politician than the retiring and unapproachable Lord Salisbury, who led the Unionist coalition from Hatfield House. He realised that the Constitution had become democratic, and that the public opinion with which ministers were concerned was now represented not by the gossip of the clubs of Pall Mall and St James's Street but by the opinions of skilled workers in the factories of Birmingham and the mines of South Wales. Essentially the task of a politician was to persuade the "People with a capital P" to give him and his policies their support.

The most obvious reason for the change was the progressive extension of the franchise. People who have the vote have to be persuaded. It must be remembered, however, that the process of persuasion can be intelligent only if the people are intelligent. If they are so ignorant of political problems that they can be stampeded by slogans or specious promises or allegations of unknown terrors, or if they do not see that acquiescence in bribery and corruption is to take part in a conspiracy to establish tyranny, a wide franchise is merely an invitation to corrupt demagogy. It would be easy to produce examples from other countries, and readers of *Mein Kampf* will be aware that the technique of the Nazi party, before Hitler obtained power, was based on the assumption that people were sheep who could be driven anywhere by lies and corruption. In Great Britain, this problem has never attained considerable proportions because the franchise in fact lagged behind political education, and the difficulty has been that whole sections of the population capable of taking part in democratic government have until recently been excluded from it. There have been recent examples of attempts to produce a mass stampede; but direct bribery and corruption have been abolished simply because it is too costly and difficult to corrupt a wide and intelligent electorate.

It is not too much to say that, in Great Britain, government by opinion, or "truckling to a multitude", arose because of the extension of political education rather than because of the extension of the franchise. A vocal opinion can mould policy even where it cannot be expressed on the hustings or in the ballot box. For instance, nothing could be more unrepresentative than the so-called representative system in Scotland between the Union in 1707 and the first Reform Act in 1832. The Scottish members of the House of Commons were chosen by corrupt oligarchies, usually under the control of the King. Accordingly, the Government had the forty-five Scottish members in its pocket. Since the Government was chosen on account of conditions in the House of Commons, where the English element was dominant, it might be assumed that in the eighteenth century the inevitable consequence of the Scottish franchise (laid down, be it noted, by the Scottish Parliament before its demise) was a permanent injustice to Scotland. The contrary was the case because, though the Scottish members were always "King's friends", they were also Scots. The price of their continued allegiance was justice to Scotland. It was not they, however, who determined what was justice to Scotland, but the vocal opinion of Scotland: and this was very wide, because the Presbyterian system in the Kirk had taught large numbers of the Scottish people to argue about and take part in the consideration of public questions, and generally the educational system (under the influence of the Kirk) was far better in Scotland than in England (where the Church was antagonistic to education and was itself a close oligarchy). The Scottish artisan, for instance, had influence on British policy in relation to Scotland long before the English artisan had any influence on British policy in relation to England.

Nevertheless, there were signs even in England towards the end of the century that a wider political education was developing. Pitt won his election in 1784 not merely because all the electioneering resources of the Crown were placed at his disposal (including the forty-five Scottish seats), but also because the spectacle of the great Chatham's son defying a parliamentary majority appealed to the middle classes, enfranchised and unenfranchised alike. Wilberforce deliberately appealed to the "conscience" of the unenfranchised middle classes in order to force the abolition of the slave trade through a Parliament where the West India interest was strong. The Whigs were induced to adopt reform in 1830 simply because there was a vocal public opinion which demanded it. Cobden and Bright, in their attack on the Corn Laws, went even further. They appealed to the working classes, who were still not enfranchised but who were beginning to have opinions of their own, with the result that, at the moment of famine, a majority for repealing the Corn Laws was found in a Parliament most of whose members had been elected to maintain them. The explanation of these and many other examples is that no person ever thinks out public policies from first principles. He does not collect all the literature from Plato and Aristotle onwards in order to find out whether there should be a limitation of the hours of work in a factory. The member for a pocket borough was, of course, concerned primarily with the opinions of his patron; but both patron and member had their opinions formed for them by contact with others. What was said in the tap-room in the county town was of far more direct importance than anything in Adam Smith; though something of what Adam Smith said became the talk of the saloon bar when the price of corn went rocketing upwards.

Naturally, when a large section of opinion becomes politically conscious it begins to demand the franchise as a right. Soon the opinion prevails, as it prevailed in 1832, that an extension of the right to vote is necessary. If at that time a political party thinks that it can secure advantage by adopting the public opinion as its own, the result will be a Reform Act again, as in 1832. Nevertheless, the immediate result of such an Act is not very great. None of the franchise reforms of the nineteenth century produced an immediate change in the membership of the House of Commons or in the policies of parties. If the balance of power is shifted, as it was in 1832 and 1867, there are ultimate effects, though they are incalculable because opinion is shifting at the same time. The importance of the changes in the franchise has, however, been overemphasised. It was at least equally important that throughout the nineteenth century the working classes were becoming politically conscious. Education in the academic sense was spread very slowly, partly of course because the middle-class oligarchy felt that education was dangerous to their political supremacy—it is one of the difficulties of the extension of democracy that democracy cannot extend without education and that it is difficult for education to extend without democracy. More important, however, is the fact that what may be called political education developed ahead of academic education. Political education is possible even among an illiterate population. The critical discussions in presbyteries was probably more important than the direct educational activities of the Presbyterian Kirk. In England and Wales the work of the Church schools and the dissenting academies began to spread downwards, though it never went very far or very deep until the State assumed control. More was done, in fact, by the very practical training produced by mechanics' institutes, the working-men's clubs, the trade unions and the co-operative societies. The effect of these influences was cumulative, because ordinary social intercourse is the most fruitful means for the spread of ideas. Perhaps the Anti-Corn Law League addressed only a minority of the population, but its ideas spread around the factories and were the common talk of the pubs. The cotton operative who could read what Disraeli said to Gladstone was the source of information, no doubt garbled, for a dozen. The progress of political education by these means during the course of the nineteenth century is obvious to anyone who has studied something of its history.

Universal education, a popular press and the wireless have now provided Great Britain with what is, comparatively, an instructed electorate. It is true that few electors have any expert knowledge of anything outside their own jobs: but this is as noticeable in the college common-room as it is in the factory. Nor has our educational system given equal opportunities to all classes. What is needed, however, is not so much knowledge as plain common sense, the ability to seize the point of an argument when it is presented in an elementary fashion. If the State had to decide nice points in the theory of knowledge or consider the composition of matter, it could do no more than leave the question to its philosophers and scientists. Fortunately, the general questions of public policy are not of this order, and for those aspects of it, such as the precise relationship between a currency and its gold backing, the ordinary individual usually has enough sense to rely on the experts. There is of course a possibility that attractive and specious arguments on technical matters—such as the nature of credit—will induce the common man to override the expert in the expert's own field; but, generally, the ordinary man will not listen to a complicated argument, and he is more concerned with the ends than the means.

Nor must it be thought that public opinion considers policy from a wholly detached and impartial angle. The ordinary individual is concerned with the general tendency as it affects himself, his family and his friends. A little political education soon convinces him that he has an interest in the welfare of the community as a whole, and in any case there is a mass of sentiment which induces altruism. The income-tax payer may rush to pay his tax because he thinks that the interest of the community requires it; the old age pensioner may send a shilling to the Chancellor of the Exchequer. Volunteers for the public service, at considerable loss and inconvenience to themselves, can always be obtained. Similarly, the individual considers the welfare of the community when he casts his vote: but he considers it in the background of his own interests. The landowner thought that the Corn Laws provided the backbone of the State, while the industrialist considered that they hindered the increase in the State's wealth and, of course, in his own. In the last resort, most people are prepared to sacrifice their own interest for that of the community; but often they see no reason why they should not gain what they can, and perhaps even more often they assume that their interest and the interest of the community are one. It is to be expected that a business man will object to the transfer of his profitable business to the State, though it is not inevitable that he should object to the transfer of other businesses—for instance, the banking business. It is equally to be expected that the worker should be anxious for higher wage rates and better conditions in his own trade, though not necessarily in other trades—because the effect may be to increase the cost of living. In practice, however, business men combine in trade associations for their mutual protection, and workers combine in trade unions for their mutual protection. This being the dominant conflict of opinion in ordinary times, the result is shown in the support of different political parties. The alignment is never precise, however; and, in particular, not all the workers are agreed that the policy of the Labour party is that best suited to the interests of the country and of themselves. In addition, there is a large body of individuals outside the two interest groups, sometimes moving in one way and sometimes in another.

Nor must this or any other cause necessarily produce irreconcilable opposition. Great Britain is a small island with a very homogeneous population. People do not think of themselves primarily as English, Scots or Welsh. The sting has long ago been taken out of religious controversy. The population is so closely interdependent that there is little economic agitation on a regional basis, as there sometimes is in a large country like the United States. There are class divisions and (what is often the same thing) economic divisions, but they are not wide or deep. We are a closely-knit economic unit, with a large measure of common interests and a long patriotic tradition. Consequently, the elements of agreement are much more important than the elements of disagreement. There is always a common public opinion which has agreed about principles, and the divergences are more about methods than about objects.

It is, nevertheless, over these differences that political debate ranges. The Constitution must provide some means for their resolution. The classic theory of democracy assumes that, because the differences are in the main the consequences of divergences in individual interest, the only way to resolve them is to take the majority opinion. The argument need not be based on "the greatest happiness of the greatest number". The intelligent individual realises that the whole is greater than the part, and that the majority gains more from the collaboration of the minority than from its suppression. Moreover, majorities become minorities and, if there is a tradition of suppression, become the victims of tyranny in their turn. What is asserted is that one man's opinion on public policy is no better than another's. The expert knows only a little about something, and is no more entitled to decide a general policy than any other person.

This is the argument for the principle of "one man (or woman), one vote". No principle is ever carried out completely logically in the British Constitution, and this principle is no exception. Every British subject of full age resident in a constituency has a vote in respect of his residence: but some people have additional qualifications. A professional or business man who occupies business premises of the value of £10 a year or more receives an additional vote in respect of that occupation if it is in another constituency, and so does his wife (or the husband where the occupier is a woman). Moreover, university graduates have votes for the special university constituencies. The result may be that a person may have four or even more votes. He is not entitled to use more than two of them (one of them the residential qualification) at a general election, but there is no real check. The consequence of these additional votes is that, though there are only about 26 million adults, there are 31 million registered voters.

The university constituencies are justified (if at all) by the fact that the universities return members of a special quality, persons who would not normally stand for election in an ordinary constituency, and add to the variety of ideas in the House of Commons. Frequently, however, the university constituencies return ordinary party politicians. For the business premises qualification there is no real justification at all. Business as such is not better represented, because the big industrial concerns are limited companies, and neither they nor their directors have votes as such. Nor is there any reason why business and professional men should have their political weight doubled. However, the effect is to secure additional votes for the Conservative party, and it is hardly to be expected that that party would willingly acquiesce in the abolition of its special advantage. Since the Conservative party always has a majority in the House of Lords, it is not possible for the other parties, except by a lengthy procedure, to put the simple principle into operation. When we regard a general election as an expression of public opinion, therefore, we must notice that middle class opinion is more heavily reflected in the votes cast than other sections of opinion and that, to put it in terms of parties, the Liberal or the Labour party must obtain the support of more than a majority of the electors.

§ 2. *The People's Choice*

A wide franchise is not the sole test of democracy. Germany and the Soviet Union have wide franchises. The cardinal factors of British democracy are that the character of the British Government depends essentially on the results of the last general election, that there must be a general election at least once every five years (except in war-time), and that the electors have a choice exercised freely and secretly between rival candidates advocating rival policies. These facts are significant in themselves; they differentiate British democracy from the so-called democracy of the Soviet Union and from the autocratic systems of Germany and Italy. They are even more important in their consequences. The Government stands or falls by the result of a general election. Every member of the House of Commons must seek re-election in not more than five years. Every action of the Government is done with close attention to the movements of public opinion in the country at large, and every time a member of Parliament casts a vote in the House of Commons he considers the movement of opinion in his own constituency. Nor is this all, the general election produces not only a Government but also an Opposition. Facing the Prime Minister in normal times is the Leader of the Opposition; opposite the Treasury Bench, where sit the members of His Majesty's Government, is the Front Opposition Bench, where sit the leaders of His Majesty's Opposition. The Leader of the Opposition is the alternative Prime Minister; only a slight shift in public opinion is necessary to give His Majesty's Opposition a majority in the House and so to convert them into His Majesty's Government. The result is to make the Government and the House very sensitive to public opinion. We have government by the people not merely because the people exercises a choice freely and secretly at short intervals, but also because it follows from that fact that the whole machinery of government—the House of Lords in part excepted—is keyed to public opinion. This fact will become more apparent as our exposition proceeds. For the present it is necessary to examine this popular choice, to find out how real and effective it is.

There must be a general election at least once every five years, because the law so provides. From 1715 to 1911 the maximum duration of Parliament was fixed at seven years. When the powers of the House of Lords were reduced in 1911, however, the maximum duration of Parliament was reduced to five years, because it was thought that, the effective powers of the House of Commons having increased, the majority ought to secure a renewal of its "mandate" more frequently. This rule is, however, a rule of law; and like every other rule of law it can be altered by Parliament. Unlike other rules of law, however, it cannot be altered by the House of Commons alone, because the Parliament Act, which enables the House of Commons to overrule the House of Lords after a delay of two years, specifically excepts laws extending the maximum duration of Parliament. Such a law therefore needs the consent of the House of Lords as well as of the House of Commons. In the House of Lords the Conservative party has a large permanent majority. Consequently, a Labour or Liberal Government with a majority in the House of Commons cannot extend the duration of Parliament without the consent of the Conservative Opposition. A Conservative Government with a majority in the House of Commons, or a Coalition Government (such as a "National" Government) supported by the Conservative party, would be in a more advantageous position. It would be politically very dangerous, however, to pass such a law without a very good reason. Unless it had the mass of the electors behind it, the Government would present a valuable propaganda weapon to the Opposition. Some of its supporters in the House of Commons might vote against it, and it would probably lose seats at bye-elections. Even if it maintained its majority during that Parliament, its "unconstitutional" action would be one of the great arguments against it when ultimately the general election arrived, and it is possible that it would then be almost annihilated by the electors.

The British Constitution provides no check against a Conservative Government which really intended to go "authoritarian", because a Government which has majorities in both Houses can do what it pleases through its control of the absolute authority of Parliament. It is possible that the King might intervene and exercise some of his dormant legal powers. Subject to this, we always run the risk, because we have no written Constitution limiting the power of Parliament. Even a written Constitution, however, is but a slight check—as Hitler showed in Germany—and the foundation of our democratic system rests not so much on laws as on the intention of the British people to resist by all the means in its power—including sabotage, the general strike, and if necessary civil war—attacks upon the liberties which it has won.

In fact, the duration of an existing Parliament has been extended only in extreme conditions. The Parliament of 1715, which was due to expire in 1718 under the Triennial Act of 1694, prolonged its own existence to a maximum of seven years because the Jacobite Rebellion had only just been put down, and it was feared that the conditions necessary for a free election might not be obtained. The Bill was strenuously opposed by the Opposition, but there appears to have been little opposition in the country. In any case, the conditions of to-day, under a democratic franchise, are very different. The Parliament of 1911, which was due to expire in January 1915, prolonged its life by a series of Acts until 1919—though it was eventually dissolved in November 1918—because of the conditions of war. There was then a Coalition Government in office with the support of the three main parties, and there was no effective opposition to it in either House. The present Parliament, due to expire in November 1940, has been similarly prolonged.

The Parliament Act fixes the maximum duration of Parliament at five years. It does not provide that a Parliament must last for so long. The King, who for this purpose invariably—or almost invariably—acts on the advice of the Prime Minister, may dissolve Parliament at any time. Elections are usually held more frequently than every five years. Not only does a Government defeated in the House of Commons, like the Labour Government of 1924, normally appeal to the people, but so does a new Government formed as a result of internal dissensions—such as the Conservative Government formed in 1922 through the resignation of Mr Lloyd George's Coalition Government, and the National Government formed in 1931 after the resignation of the Labour Government. Moreover, a Government which desires to set out upon a new policy will and ought to appeal for a "mandate", as Mr Baldwin appealed for a mandate for Protection in 1923. Finally, a Government naturally chooses the moment for an election most favourable to its own prospects. If it allows Parliament to expire, it may have to conduct its electioneering while it is passing through a period of temporary unpopularity. Consequently, Parliament is usually dissolved well before the expiration of its normal life. For these reasons, during the twenty years' peace between 1918 and 1939, we had not five elections but seven—in 1918, 1922, 1923, 1924, 1929, 1931 and 1935—and we should probably have had another in the autumn of 1939 if the war had not broken out.

Theoretically, the elector does not vote for a Government but for a single member—or in a few cases for two or three members. Since 1884 the practice has been to have single-member constituencies; that is, with few

Secret ballot

exceptions each constituency returns one member. The present constituencies were arranged in 1918 by impartial boundary commissions which included no politicians from any party. They were instructed to allocate one member to roughly 70,000 inhabitants, though a borough or county did not lose its separate representation if it had less than 70,000 but more than 50,000 inhabitants. Also they had to pay some attention to area, because in some rural counties—in the Highlands of Scotland, for instance—a constituency containing 70,000 inhabitants would cover an area far too large for a candidate to "nurse" or a member to represent.

There was, too, a qualification made in the case of those boroughs which had two members in 1883, and which continued to have two members both under the 1884 Act and under the 1918 Act. In such a case the borough continues to be a two-member constituency, that is, the borough is not divided, but every elector can vote for two candidates. The commissioners had no concern with the university constituencies, which were given representation on a special basis. Moreover, the number of members for Northern Ireland was reduced when the separate Parliament of Northern Ireland was created, and single-member constituencies were not always adopted.

The result is that each constituency has one member only, except in the following cases:

City of London (two members).

Blackburn, Bolton, Brighton, Derby, Norwich, Oldham, Preston, Southampton, Stockport, Sunderland and Dundee (two members each).

Antrim, Down, and Fermanagh and Tyrone (two members each).

Oxford, Cambridge and English Universities (two members each).

Scottish Universities (three members).

The fact that boundaries were drawn by impartial committees is of considerable importance, and indicates the ability of British political parties deliberately to deprive themselves of political advantages where the national interest requires it. Other countries, including some within the British Commonwealth, are familiar with "gerrymandering", whereby the party in power alters constituencies to suit its own political circumstances. Let us take by way of example a town of 150,000 electors (say 280,000 inhabitants) entitled to four members. Let us assume further that one-quarter of the electors belongs to the working class, lives in the centre of the town, and normally votes Labour, while the rest belongs to the middle class, lives in the suburbs, and normally votes Conservative. If the town is divided diagonally into four quarters, each including part of the centre as well as part of the suburbs, it will return four Conservative members. If the centre forms one constituency and the suburbs are divided into three constituencies, it will return one Labour member and three Conservatives. This of course states the problem in a form so simple that it could never possibly arise. It shows, however, that much depends on the way in which boundaries are drawn.

It is not suggested that the distribution adopted by the commissioners was entirely fair. Their task was to make such changes as were necessitated by the Act of 1918, and not completely to remodel the constituencies. On balance the arrangements favoured the Conservative party. The increase in the number of electors due to the granting of the equal franchise to women in 1928, and the great changes in the distribution of population since 1918, have made the 1918 scheme quite unrepresentative. In 1935, for instance, the Hendon Division of Middlesex had over 180,000 electors, while Bethnal Green, S.W., had less than 27,000. The successful Liberal candidate in the latter received less than one-ninth of the votes cast for the successful Conservative candidate in the former. For the most part, these changes have given the central and industrial areas an advantage over the suburbs, and have therefore benefited the Labour party, but it is still true to say that the distribution of seats favours the Conservative party, though not to the same extent as in 1918.

The single-member constituency has the advantage that it is comparatively small and enables the member to establish personal contact with large numbers of his constituents. They feel that he is their member, and he feels a personal responsibility for their welfare. It is, however, fallacious to assume that normally the electors vote for an individual. Very few of them know anything about the candidates except their party labels. The British political system differs from many other systems in that the local member is rarely the "favourite son" of the constituency. The nineteenth century used to speak of "carpet-bagger" candidates—candidates who came down to the constituency with their "carpet-bags" at the beginning of the campaign, put up at the local hostelry for a few weeks, and then went back either cheerfully to Westminster or dolefully whence they came. The term has dropped out of use, not only because carpet-bags are no longer seen, but also because nearly all candidates are carpet-baggers. They have been chosen from lists submitted by the appropriate political bodies. It is true that a Welsh constituency insists upon a Welshman, that many Scottish constituencies insist on Scotsmen, and that Oxford and Cambridge universities require that their candidates shall have been educated at the right universities. It does not often happen, however, that Muddleton is represented by a Muddletonian. The elector does not look round among his acquaintances to find out which of them is best capable of representing him in Parliament. He learns his politics in political discussion at home, in the factory, in the club; he reads the newspaper which gives him the best racing tips or which panders to his other (or his wife's) tastes, and comes to conclusions about prominent politicians and their policies from the news which it gives; he listens to the political leaders on the wireless; and he then decides which party (if any) shall receive his support.

The qualities of the candidate therefore have little to do with his choice. A very good candidate may pick up a few hundred votes by assiduous "nursing". If by chance a prominent Muddletonian does get selected, he may obtain even a couple of thousand votes which are cast for him and not for his party. A courtesy peer who has a handsome or gracious wife may be able to capitalise the snobbery of the back streets. These factors may prove important in a few constituencies, but generally speaking it is the party label that matters. This statement can be proved not merely by common experience, but also by analysis of the voting in the few double-member constituencies. Brighton, for instance, is represented by two members, and each of its electors has two votes. It may be assumed that one of the two Conservatives is more able, more popular, more persuasive than the other. Accordingly, if the electors voted for the man rather than for the party, there ought to be a substantial difference in the votes cast for the two candidates. Actually, we find that (with rare exceptions) the two Conservatives, the two Liberals and the two Labour candidates in any double-member constituency are within a couple of hundred votes of each other. That is to say, the electors have made up their minds according to the policies of the parties, and not according to the personalities of the candidates. There are occasional exceptions, and it is then invariably found that one of the candidates has some strong local "pull". For instance, he may come from a family which has been prominent in the locality for generations, or he may be a popular employer of labour in the town, or he may be a trade-union leader who has made a name for himself in national politics. This special quality may gain him an extra two thousand votes, and in some constituencies two thousand votes would be important. The number of such candidates is, however, few; and if their local "pull" is to be of any use, the constituency must be one in which the parties are almost equally balanced—because in most constituencies two thousand votes is a small proportion of the total. These conditions are not present in the great majority of constituencies. The representation of a "safe seat" is determined by the choice of the local party committee. The representation of the more doubtful constituencies is determined by two factors only, the general balance of political opinion, and the choice of the local party committee. In almost all cases it is the label and not the candidate that matters.

The consequences are important. For instance, it places a very great public responsibility upon the local party committees. For our present purpose, however, the point of interest is that the situation minimises the value of the single-member constituency. The real purpose of the election is not to give Muddleton a representative, but to enable all the Muddletons together to choose a Government by choosing a majority in the House of Commons. Individuals in Muddleton want some representative to put their special complaints to ministers—John Smith wants to know why he has not had a pension; Herbert Thomas thinks that "the means test man" has not given him enough unemployment assistance; the Chamber of Commerce wants a late delivery of letters; the local trades council thinks that some assistance should be given to local industry—but any active member can do this, and he need know very little about Muddleton. What is important is that the single-member constituencies shall produce the right balance of political forces. Actually, this is just what they often fail to do.

In the first place, the minority is completely unrepresented. In Romford, in 1935, nearly 56,000 electors voted for the successful Labour candidate, but 47,000 electors voted for the Conservative. This was to some extent balanced in the neighbouring constituency of South-East Essex, where less than a thousand votes separated the successful Conservative candidate and the unsuccessful Labour candidate. In fact, taking Essex as a whole, it was the Labour electors who were under-represented, since they obtained one seat for 135,000 votes, whereas the Conservatives obtained six seats for 193,000 votes. In the rest of the county constituencies in the South of England the disparity was even greater, because the Labour party, in spite of its hundreds of thousand of votes, did not obtain a single seat. Taking the country as a whole, the Government obtained 406 seats in contested elections through 11,810,158 votes, or one seat for about 29,000 votes. The Opposition, on the other hand, obtained 169 seats in contested elections through 10,106,896 votes, or one seat for about 60,000 votes.

The consequence is that representation in the House of Commons may give a totally inadequate picture of the state of opinion in the country. The general impression which most people have of the general election in 1918, for instance, is that Mr Lloyd George's Coalition swept the country with such slogans as "Hang the Kaiser", "Make Germany Pay", and "A Land fit for Heroes to live in". The Coalition Government had 525 supporters in the House of Commons, while Opposition parties had 181 (including 73 from the Sinn Fein party, which was over-represented). If each party had been represented proportionately, however, the Government would have had 395 supporters and the Opposition 311 supporters. The actual majority for making Germany pay, and the rest, was 344; it ought to have been 84. It is possible to assert, and it has been asserted, that the Treaty of Versailles would have been very different if Mr Lloyd George had not had so many "hard-faced colonels" watching his every movement and protesting vehemently at every suggestion of clemency to the defeated enemy.

This is a serious accusation, and one which could not have been made so strongly if the House of Commons had not rejected certain of the proposals of the Speaker's Conference on whose main recommendations the new franchise laws of 1918 were based. The Conference had agreed that in every single-member constituency the alternative vote should be used. This means that the elector, instead of plumping for one candidate by putting a cross against his name, would place the candidates in order of preference. If no candidate secured an absolute majority, the first preferences given for the lowest candidate would be ignored, and the second preferences distributed. Suppose, for instance, that in counting the first preference the following result had been obtained:

Cholmondeley (Co.Un.)	25,000
Cadbury (Lib.)	20,000
Jones (Lab.)	15,000

We may assume that most of the Labour voters had given the Liberal candidate as their second choice; but suppose that 2000 had chosen the Coalition-Unionist and 3000 had not given a second choice at all. The result would then be:

Cadbury (Lib.)	30,000
Cholmondeley (Co.Un.)	27,000

This result is alleged to be fairer, because a majority of the electors preferred the Liberal to the Coalition candidate.

In addition, the Speaker's Conference proposed that large towns with more than two representatives should be formed into single constituencies, and that voting should be based on the principle of proportional representation by the single transferable vote. As in the case of the alternative vote, each voter would mark the candidates in order of preference. The difference is, however, that whereas under the alternative vote system each voter has one vote for one member, under proportional representation there would be at least three members, and each elector would have only one vote, which would be transferred in the order of his preferences.

Let us suppose that a town which, under a single-member system, would have returned three Coalition candidates had formed a single constituency under proportional representation. The first preferences might be divided as follows:

First Count

Cholmondeley (Co.Un.)	85,000
Cadbury (Lib.)	65,000
Berkeley (Co.Lib.)	50,000
Jones (Labour)	45,000
Fry (Lib.)	20,000
Chamberlain (Co.Un.)	15,000
	280,000

Three members have to be elected; and there are 280,000 votes. If any candidate receives 70,001 votes he *must* be elected, because $3 \times 70,001 = 210,003$. The fourth candidate would thus have at most 60,997 votes. Accordingly, Cholmondeley has 14,999 votes to spare, and if we want to give equal value to every vote, we must divide this surplus among the other candidates. Taking now Cholmondeley's *second* preferences, we find them divided among the other candidates in a certain proportion. Dividing 14,999[1] votes in that proportion, we reach the following:

Second Count

Cholmondeley (Co.Un.)		70,001

Cadbury (Lib.)	65,000 + 200	= 65,200
Berkeley (Co.Lib.)	50,000 + 1000	= 51,000
Jones (Lab.)	45,000 + 100	= 45,100
Chamberlain (Co.Un.)	15,000 + 13,599	= 28,599
Fry (Lib.)	20,000 + 100	= 20,100
		280,000

On this second count, no candidate except Cholmondeley gets 70,001, so we must take the bottom candidate and divide up his second preferences (or the third preferences of the 100 people who voted for Cholmondeley first and Fry second). The result is as follows:

Third Count

Cholmondeley (Co.Un.)		70,001

Cadbury (Lib.)	65,200 + 14,000	= 79,200
Berkeley (Co.Lib.)	51,000 + 5000	= 56,000
Jones (Lab.)	45,100 + 500	= 45,600
Chamberlain (Co.Un.)	28,599 + 600	= 29,199
		280,000

Cadbury has now more than the quota, so we distribute his surplus votes as we did for Cholmondeley, with the following result:

Fourth Count

Cholmondeley (Co.Un.)		70,001
Cadbury (Lib.)		70,001

Berkeley (Co.Lib.)	56,000 + 4000	= 60,000
Jones (Lab.)	45,600 + 5000	= 50,600
Chamberlain (Co.Un.)	29,199 + 199	= 29,398
		280,000

[1] For simplicity of exposition, it is assumed that each voter makes a full list of preferences. Actually, many would prefer simply to vote for one member, or for Coalition members or Liberal members only.

This time, Chamberlain must go, so we divide his votes according to their next preferences, and reach this conclusion:

Fifth Count

Cholmondeley (Co.Un.)	70,001
Cadbury (Lib.)	70,001

Berkeley (Co.Lib.)	$60,000 + 29,000 =$	89,000
Jones (Lab.)	$50,600 + 398$ $\ \ =$	50,998
		280,000

The final result is, then, that this constituency, which would have been represented by three Coalition members if it had been divided up, is represented by two Coalition supporters and a member of the Liberal Opposition. Moreover, a slight increase in the popularity of the Labour party would have given Jones a quota and would have secured his election instead of Berkeley.

This system was recommended by the Speaker's Conference, but it was rejected by the House of Commons. It was restored by the House of Lords, which however rejected the alternative vote. Eventually the two Houses reached a compromise under which both the alternative vote and the single transferable vote disappeared, except that the single transferable vote was retained for the university constituencies returning two or more members. There was also a provision by which commissioners were to prepare a scheme for the election of one hundred members on the principle of proportional representation. No action was ever taken on it, and it was repealed in 1927 as obsolete.

The alternative vote and proportional representation are at first sight so attractive that the case for them appears to be unanswerable. It may be noted that if proportional representation is good for the towns, or for one hundred constituencies, it is good for the whole country, and in that case there is no need for the alternative vote, which is admitted to be a device less satisfactory than proportional representation. There is, however, this qualification, that towns are compact constituencies, whereas some rural constituencies cover large areas. For proportional representation to work effectively, there ought to be at least three members to a constituency, so that, for instance, Inverness, Ross and Cromarty, and possibly Caithness and Sutherland as well, would form a single constituency covering between two and four million acres.

Let us first consider the alternative vote. Its first result would be to encourage three-cornered or four-cornered contests, because a candidate who could not hope to win on a majority or a plurality[1] would hope to win on second preferences. To come down to practical politics, it would have encouraged the Labour party to put up more candidates before 1914, because Labour candidates would expect to receive the second preferences of Liberal voters; and it would have encouraged the Liberal party to put up more candidates since 1918, because Liberal candidates would expect to get the second preferences of both Conservative and Labour voters. In the second place, and as a consequence, the occasions on which the Government had not a majority in the House of Commons would be more frequent. It is possible that no party would have had a majority in 1922, 1923, 1924 and 1929—though of course there would have been more elections, because the Conservatives would probably not have had a majority in 1924.

In the third place, it would demand bargains between the parties before an election and, if it resulted in no party having a majority, bargains in the House or else Coalition Governments. There would be, too, bargains between individual candidates and a process of angling for second preferences by means of election pledges.

[1] This convenient American term is used to cover the case of a candidate who is elected because he has most votes, but not an absolute majority of the votes.

This was described in 1918 as "log-rolling". In one of the debates in the House of Commons, Sir George Younger showed what would have been the result of the elections of 1910 if there had been compacts between the various parties, and the electors had obeyed party requests as to the distribution of their second preferences. It is much more interesting to take the election of 1929, where more than half the members secured election on a plurality. The result may be tabulated as follows:[1]

	Cons.	Lib.	Lab.	Others	Government
Actual result	260	59	287	9	Labour (minority)
Cons.-Lib. "deal"	368	76	162	9	Conservative
Cons.-Lab. "deal"	291	19	276	9	Conservative (minority or Coalition
Lab.-Lib. "deal"	112	139	354	9	Labour

This is far too simplified to be accurate: many electors would refuse to follow the party decision; and the working would be complicated by local "deals". The table does show, however, that elections might be determined not so much by the electors as by the party managers.

In the fourth place, the alternative vote system equates the second preferences given by those who voted for the candidates with fewest first preferences, with the first preferences given to the others. Clearly, a first preference is more important than a second preference. The result is to secure the election not of the candidate who is approved by the largest group, but of *one* of the candidates who is not seriously objected to. This is shown by dividing out the second preferences in the case of each candidate in turn.[2]

---

[1] Where the "deal" would not have applied, the actual result is taken.
[2] Thus
  (1) First preferences only:

Cholmondeley (Cons.)	20,000
Cadbury (Lib.)	15,000
Jones (Lab.)	10,000

In one of the House of Commons debates, Sir F. E. Smith (afterwards the first Lord Birkenhead) said that the previous speaker had given sixteen reasons against proportional representation. Some of the reasons usually stated against it can be dismissed in a few words. It clearly requires multiple constituencies, and thus would sometimes necessitate constituencies large in area. On the whole, however, the United Kingdom is densely populated, and multiple constituencies even in the north of Scotland would be small compared with some of the single-member constituencies in Canada or Australia. Again, it is argued that the contact between members and constituents would be less close—undoubtedly it would be, but this is not very important, partly because the elector really votes for a party, and partly because, in many cases, he would be able to communicate with a member with whose politics he sympathises. The present Communist member for West Fife really charges himself with the complaints of all Communists in the country, and many electors write to members belonging to other constituencies, simply because they would rather write to the devil than to their own member. Another objection is that proportional representation is too complicated—but it is complicated for the returning officer, not for the voter, who merely has to write numbers against the candidates' names. Finally, proportional representa-

(2) Divide Jones's second preferences:

Cadbury (Lib.)	23,000
Cholmondeley (Cons.)	22,000

(3) Divide Cadbury's second preferences:

Cholmondeley (Cons.)	29,000
Jones (Lab.)	16,000

(4) Divide Cholmondeley's second preferences:

Cadbury (Lib.)	33,000
Jones (Lab.)	12,000

The only certain result is that the electors do not want Jones. Under the alternative vote system Cadbury is elected, but only one-third of the electorate really wants him to be elected. In actual practice, of course, the result would be determined by "log-rolling".

tion cannot be applied to bye-elections; but that is no reason for not applying it to general elections.

Proportional representation has, however, one consequence, which can be regarded as good or bad according to one's point of view. Our present system helps to maintain the two-party system; and when that system breaks up, as during the growth of the Labour party, it is a strong force towards compelling its return. Whether this is desirable or not depends on whether the two-party system is good or bad. Reasons are given in the next chapter for suggesting that it is good; but many disagree, particularly those who belong to middle parties which are being crushed out. It is significant that, while the Liberal party has favoured proportional representation consistently since 1918, neither the Conservative party nor the Labour party has given any support—though opinion was very divided in 1917–18, when party lines were fluid, and some Conservative and Labour members support the Proportional Representation Society.

In order to be elected under the present system, a candidate must secure the highest number of votes. If he starts with a party "label" he is certain of the party votes. The elector has made up his mind to vote for one party or another. What he is doing in fact is to choose that party which he wishes to see forming a government. In 1935 his choice lay between the National Government and the Labour party. No other party had enough candidates to secure a majority, and of 22 million votes cast, over 20 million were cast for the Government or for the Labour party. The elector has one vote, and he naturally wishes to use it to support the existing government or to put another in its place. This is partly the cause, but mainly the consequence of the two-party system. Because the elector wants to help choose a government, therefore he votes for the government or the chief opposition party. But he wants to help choose a government because we have the two-party system and because he has only one vote.

If his vote is transferable, however, other motives come into operation. He not only wants to bring one party *in*; he also wants to keep one party *out*. Thus, most Conservatives would prefer a Liberal to a Labour member: and most Labour voters would prefer a Liberal to a Conservative. Accordingly, three-corner fights would operate to the benefit of the Liberal party. The result might be—it probably would have been at any election since 1918 except that of 1931—that no party would have a majority. Moreover, this would not be a temporary phase, as we thought it in 1924 and 1929, but a permanent feature. Once this had happened, and we had departed from the two-party system, the electors would no longer vote for a government but for a group. The main buttress of the two-party system would be destroyed, and not only would later preferences be distributed, but so would first preferences. Further, the groups would not be limited to the Conservative, Liberal and Labour parties. Any section of opinion which could secure enough preferences in any constituency—and electors would vote according to their special interests and not according to their view as to what government should be in power—would put up a candidate. Proportional representation has therefore been described as a movement for the encouragement of "sects". Our present system induces sectional opinions to find representation within a party, or to secure their acceptance by members of both parties. Under proportional representation they would be the basis of separate parties.

We should thus have a House of Commons divided not into Government and Opposition but into *blocs*. Every government would be a coalition. Moreover, it would not be the kind of coalition which we had in 1918–22 or have had since 1931. The parties in those coalitions have had separate organisations, but they have fought elections as units. The government candidatures have been divided up by agreement among the parties. A Coalition Liberal did not oppose a Coalition Unionist; nor did a Liberal National oppose a Conservative. Under proportional representation we should have much less stable coalitions, without electoral pacts, except on a temporary basis. The elector would vote for candidates or parties not, as he does now, for a government.

The swing of the pendulum:
Government majorities since 1832

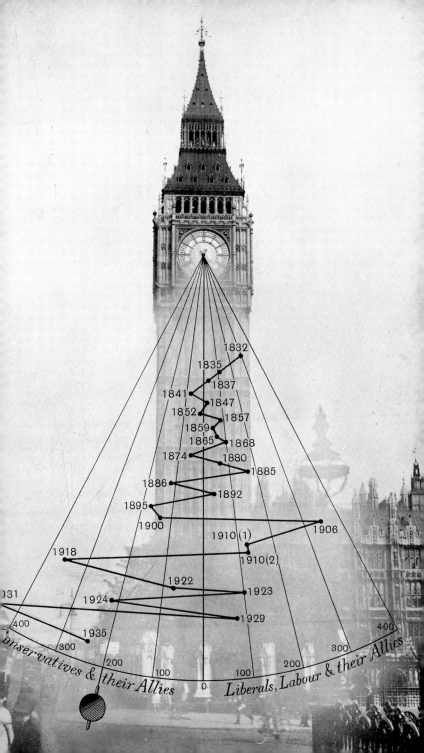

1832
1835
1837
1841
1847
1852
1857
1859
1868
1865
1880
1874
1885
1886
1892
1895
1900
1906
1910 (1)
1918
1910 (2)
1922
1923
1924
1929
1931
1935

400 300 200 100 0 100 200 300 400

Conservatives & their Allies   Liberals, Labour & their Allies

CHAPTER II

GOVERNMENT BY PARTY

§ 1. *The Polity of Parties*

John Stuart Mill wrote a book on *Representative Government* without mentioning parties. A realistic survey of the British Constitution to-day must begin and end with parties and discuss them at length in the middle. There are some who deplore the influence of parties. They assert that the tasks of government are too urgent and complicated to be the subject of partisan controversy. They would wish Parliament to be a "Council of State" to consider, free from party bias, the nature of the problems that beset the community and the solutions that might be devised to meet them. They want to pool the intelligence of the nation, not to divide it into two parts by the parliamentary gangway. They dislike debate when action is what is required. They urge statesmen to "pull together", and not to have bow side cry "forward", while stroke side cries "back".

It is an attractive picture. The difficulty, to continue the rowing metaphor, is that there is no agreement as to who shall be cox. One cannot expect either side to pull with a will if cox announces his intention of steering the boat over the weir: and the difficulty in politics is that there are different views as to where the weirs are to be found. The assumption upon which democracy is based is that inevitably there are differing views as to the policy which a State should follow. No honest man is entitled to assume that one policy is better than another; all that he can say is that he thinks that one is better. It will generally be found that the critic who asserts that parties are unnecessary has a belief in the rightness of his own opinion so profound that he does not realise that it is a partisan opinion. He wants a "Council of State" to carry out his policy. <u>The true democrat has a suspicion that he may not always be right</u>. He is therefore tolerant of other people's opinions. Moreover, since there is no court of appeal by which a controversy can be determined, he acquiesces in the system of counting votes. A majority may not be best capable of determining what is good for humanity, but it is probably better able than the minority to determine what is good for the majority; if the majority is also tolerant, it will not in the process injure the minority more than it can help.

Tolerance in this country is a principle of long standing. It has developed gradually from the struggles of the seventeenth century. It has been carried out in the laws; but it is still more an attitude of mind. It is, however, not tolerance alone that makes democratic government work. With us, the majority is not permanent. It is based upon differing views of personal and national interest, views which are susceptible of change and, in a sufficient number of persons, do change from time to time. Not only do opinions fluctuate, but they fluctuate sometimes violently, and the "swing of the pendulum" is a familiar feature of British politics. Consequently, parties can and do appeal to reason. Majorities are unstable, and the Opposition of to-day is the Government of to-morrow. This important fact must not be forgotten, for it enables the minority to submit peacefully and even cheerfully to the fulfilment of the policy of the majority. It would be quite different if the minority were always a minority, if it were liable to oppression by the majority, and if in no circumstances could its views prevail.

Political parties founded on factors which are not matters of opinion are a danger. I can be Conservative to-day and Socialist to-morrow. Both parties angle for my support, and therefore are careful of my interests. Apart from the fact that toleration extends to Jews as to Gentiles, a government will not oppress Jews so long as Jewish voters support both parties. Similarly, there will be no "injustice to Scotland" so long as Scots vote Conservative, Liberal and Labour and not Scottish Nationalist. If, however, Englishmen vote for an English party and Scots for a Scottish party, either Scotland will be oppressed or the Union will be destroyed. To say this is not necessarily to blame the Irish; the Irish movement arose while there was discrimination on the ground of religion; and it does not necessarily follow that the Union ought to have been preserved either in respect of Ireland or in respect of Scotland. All that is implied in the present argument is that the party system will not work unless it is based on factors of opinion which can change. A Conservative Government might persuade me to become a Conservative overnight. It cannot change my ancestry, my language, my caste (if I had one), my religion, or even my economic status.

Nor does it follow that these factors are not important in the choice of party. We shall see that some of them have had profound influence on the development and bias of the British parties: but no party capable of forming a government has been founded essentially on any unchangeable factor or on any combination of such factors. British parties are catholic in the true sense. Neither in their organisation nor in the implications of their policy have they excluded any person from supporting them, on grounds of ancestry, religion or even economic status. The Conservative party is not all capitalists, nor is the Labour party made up entirely of workers.

This catholicity has enabled the parties to be wide in the scope of their policies. Each party contains members and attracts supporters of differing opinions. It has enabled us to differentiate between opposition and obstruction. The Irish Nationalist party obstructed because it insisted on its own programme. Other parties oppose because they want to appeal to the people to support their own programme. Only occasionally—as with the Parliament Bill of 1911 and the Trade Unions and Trade Disputes Bill of 1927—does a British party obstruct; and it does so then because the party in opposition believes that the Government is taking an unfair advantage of its temporary majority. It is not true, therefore, that the parties are pulling in different directions. Only one party is pulling, and the other is merely criticising. The Opposition warns; and in warning it seeks to change opinion. It says that certain consequences will follow; if these consequences do follow, and they appear undesirable to a few hundred thousand electors, the Government will be overthrown and policy will be diverted along different lines.

Moreover, this same catholicity, this fact that Government and Opposition appeal to a few hundred thousand electors, produces the consequence that the actual division of opinion is not very precise. There are fundamentally opposed views in the House of Commons, but they are generally not majority opinions on either side. Bagehot long ago pointed out that the differences between Liberals and Conservatives were not great. It is true that he was writing only twenty years after Peel had adopted Cobden's policy by repealing the Corn Laws, and only a year or so after Palmerston governed the country with the tacit consent of the Conservative party.

There have been issues which have fiercely divided the country, like Home Rule in 1886 and the Parliament Bill in 1910. Yet a Conservative majority gave Home Rule and much more to Ireland, and Bonar Law sat at Asquith's right hand before the Parliament of 1910 expired. Nor has the rise of the Labour party and the demand for socialism made much difference. We are all collectivists now. Sir Stafford Cripps does not agree with Lord Londonderry, but there is much less difference between Mr Attlee and Mr Chamberlain. On this subject more must be said; but it is part of the explanation of the fact that the British party system does not prevent government. It makes it more consonant with public opinion.

No doubt parliamentary opposition slows up the governmental machine. It would be easier to carry out a policy if it were not subject to criticism. The time between decision and the first stage of execution is much longer than in a dictatorship, except when rapid execution is really urgent—and then the British machine is the most rapid in the world, for quite different reasons. It is often said that a democracy necessarily works more slowly than a dictatorship. It must be remembered, however, that the process between the discovery of the initial fault or complaint and the remedying of that fault is necessarily a complicated one. It has to come up through the official strata until it reaches the point at which a decision can be taken. There follows the period of decision (which may be longer with a single dictator than with a Cabinet). Then comes the issue of the necessary orders; and finally there is another process of percolation through the official strata until the remedy is applied. The process is much the same in all countries. If there is a legislature, however, it sometimes happens that no orders can be issued until legislation has been passed; and here the party system may interpose delay. The other parts of the procedure may, however, be shorter; and generally they are shorter in Great Britain than in Germany, for example. Moreover, the parliamentary system has the great advantage that a particular fault may be brought to the top stratum by a question or a debate in Parliament. The German citizen can reach Herr Hitler only through an immense bureaucracy. Any British subject can reach the Cabinet at once through his member. Further, the policy decided upon depends in all countries upon the currents of public opinion. In a dictatorship it is most difficult to ascertain them, particularly if the press is muzzled. In Great Britain opinion is vocal, and primarily in Parliament. The Cabinet, so to speak, goes to Parliament every afternoon and asks if there are any complaints; and at once from the Opposition there arises a chorus of "Yes, Sir".

§ 2. *The Character of the Parties*

British parties, like the British Constitution, have a long history. Like the British Constitution, too, they have drawn from that history traditions whose influences are of deep importance. A constitution is not a framework of laws, but a tissue of dynamic relationships. A party does not consist of members and a programme, but a whole complex of traditions, loyalties and ideas. Government, as British people understand it, cannot be studied as anatomy, but as biology. The division of opinion which gave rise to parties is commonly dated from 1660, but it really arose out of the Reformation. The Tory party was for centuries the "Church party", the party which emphasised the unity of English Protestantism in the Church of England against the religious anarchy of the "sects". The two sections of opinion could combine against papacy, as they did in the revolutions of 1642 and 1688, but they parted as soon as papacy was no longer an issue. Moreover, the differences of Churchman and Puritan became, through the revolution of 1642, the differences of Royalist and Republican, or Cavalier and Roundhead, or Prerogative and Parliament. The Tory party supported "Church and King", the Whigs religious toleration (except for papists) and Parliament. The revolution of 1688 weakened the Tories because, though they supported it in their opposition to papacy, its principles caused a conflict between Church and King. The Whigs regarded the revolution as their own because it established the supremacy of Parliament. The Tories found their allegiance divided between the Hanoverian head of the Church and the papist "King across the water".

The decline of religious fervour among the upper classes, the defeat of Charles Edward Stuart at Culloden, and the accession as George III of a Hanoverian who "gloried in the name of Briton" rallied Toryism. The Younger Pitt began as a Whig, but became in effect leader of the Tories when he was made Prime Minister in 1784. The basis of the modern party division, however, was produced by the French Revolution. The conservative Whigs under the Duke of Portland joined Pitt "to maintain the Constitution and save the country". Burke, who led the way, became the philosopher of conservatism; and Charles James Fox and Charles Grey led, or failed to lead, the remnant of the Whigs in the defence of liberalism against the long conservative reaction. Pitt gave way to Addington, Addington to Grenville, Grenville to Portland, Portland to Perceval, Perceval to Liverpool, Liverpool to Canning, and Canning to the Duke of Wellington.

In this period conservatism obtained its association with imperialism. Pitt and Burke were for the French war, Fox against it. Antagonism to the war was, it was alleged, unpatriotic. So patriotism or imperialism became the special attribute of conservatism. In the long contests with Napoleon and in the even more difficult contest with the social conditions produced by the war and the Industrial Revolution, patriotism and repression naturally went hand in hand. There was, indeed, another England. It had burst into politics from time to time, as in the Westminster election of 1780. For the most part, however, it was not represented in Parliament. It consisted not only of the new industrial proletariat and all the radicals from the writers of seditious pamphlets to the Benthamites, but also of the capitalists operating the developing factory system. These last were differentiated from the proletariat only by their growing wealth. They were, for the most part, nonconformist and therefore liberal. They disliked the restrictive laws that were designed to keep up rents and, therefore, the costs of production. They disliked even more the Church-going Tory councils controlling the towns that industry was causing to split their bounds. It was this England which compelled the Whig and Canningite (Tory) Government which at last came into power under Earl Grey in 1830 to introduce and carry the Reform Bill.

The new middle class did not at once come to power. The great Whig families were still predominant in the Reform ministry. It was not the Whigs, but Cobden and Bright and their manufacturing and farming allies in the Anti-Corn Law League who, assisted by a famine in Ireland, compelled Peel to repeal the Corn Laws and split his party.

The Whigs and the Peelites formed the Liberal party which governed almost without a break from 1846 to 1874. It took its liberalism from Fox and from the great band of propagandists who used their pens to fight reaction after Waterloo. Its free-trade principles and its individualism came from Adam Smith by way of Cobden and Peel. Its dislike of "foreign adventures" was half suppressed so long as the Canningite Palmerston held sway, but became dominant when Gladstone's authority was enough to swing the balance to Cobdenism. Its social reform came from Bentham, though it was never very prominent at this stage.

Facing it was the Conservative party, carefully nursed by Disraeli after the surgical operation of 1846. The "country party", the country gentlemen whose names Disraeli rolled off in a succulent page of his *Lord George Bentinck*, were edged away from tariffs and rents and began to think in terms of royalties and building values. Disraeli (who had had a short political experience as a radical) knew about the other England which was still not represented, the England he described in *Sybil*, the England that hated the new poor law, which had for a time been attracted by the Charter, which had cheered Cobden's attack on the high price of bread. This "nation" had been the care of Lord Shaftesbury and other Tory philanthropists who sought to reform factory conditions against the resistance of the manufacturers who supported the Liberal party. The new paternalism which seemed appropriate owes less to Disraeli than is commonly assumed. It owes far more to administrators like Sir Edwin Chadwick and Dr Southwood Smith, who assisted the development of local services; and it owes even more to the forgotten councillors of Liverpool, Manchester, Bradford and Birmingham who drove this special legislation through an apathetic Parliament. Nevertheless, Disraeli "dished the Whigs" by extending the franchise to the better paid urban workers, and he made enough speeches on the social question to lay the basis for "Tory democracy". In one respect only did Disraeli carry on the Tory tradition. He took over from Palmerston the banner of "mighty England". He insisted that British opinion should count in the councils of Europe. Under him British expansion proceeded in Asia and Africa. He left to Gladstone in 1880 a legacy of "little wars" and "prancing proconsuls" which the Liberals did not dispose of as the Conservatives would have wished.

In spite of this new Disraelian Conservatism, the division between the two parties was largely on an economic or "class" basis. This does not mean, and it has never meant in British politics, that the upper middle class was entirely Conservative and the lower middle class and such sections of the working class as had the vote were entirely Liberal. If it had been so the party system could not have worked. The general appeal of the Liberals was, however, to the manufacturers and the workers and to what was almost the same thing, the nonconformists. The Conservative party appealed to the *rentiers* and the Church of England. Two factors, however, somewhat changed the situation. As other forms of capital developed, the importance of landed property diminished. While the manufacturers were still in large part Liberal, the new class of entrepreneurs, those concerned with finance generally and with internal transport, tended to become Conservatives. The second factor was even more important. The scale of capitalist enterprise developed. The manufacturer like Bright or Cobden, who worked in his shirt-sleeves with his men, was replaced by the company director, who was separated from them socially as well as in the factory. Industry became "respectable". Moreover, the process created new classes, the accountants, clerks and other "black-coated workers". In the social changes which occurred, nonconformity lost some of its appeal among the manufacturers, but spread a little among the black-coated workers. At this period the "Nonconformist Conscience" still induced Liberal votes, and the Church was still associated with Conservatism. The religious question (which was, in fact, not religious but social) lost its importance as the working class was enfranchised, because (in spite of efforts by the Evangelicals and the later nonconformists) the urban proletariat had as a whole never been harnessed by any religious body. The nonconformist conscience appears still to be strong in the Liberal party, and perhaps explains the devotion of the "Celtic fringe" to liberalism.

Home Rule completed the process of separating the parties along new class lines. Irrelevant though the issue may appear, it was a conflict between that element in liberalism which we should now call "self-determination" and the more strident nationalism which may be described (without necessarily any sinister connotation) as imperialism. It carried into the Unionist camp the last of the great Whig families under the leadership of a Cavendish, and henceforth "Society" knew few Liberals. It is true that Joseph Chamberlain went with the Whigs, presumably because his imperialism proved stronger than his radicalism; and his personal prestige was great enough to carry with him some of the radical elements in the Midlands. He thus reinforced the democratic element in the Conservative party, which had been growing since Disraeli.

The work of the Home Rule issue was strengthened by the Boer War, and the Liberal party which rose on the crest of the wave in 1905 was essentially radical. In the meantime, however, the Labour movement had come into existence. Essentially the product of the Reform Acts of 1867 and 1884, it had been made possible by the rapid development of trade unionism, especially after Disraeli's untrammelling legislation. This unionism was essentially non-political until the strikes of the 'eighties and the "judicial legislation" which found new restrictions in the common law induced sections of the movement to believe that political action was a necessary ancillary to industrial organisation. The Liberal party had never paid much attention to the "condition of

England", as Chamberlain saw when he developed the "unauthorised programme" in 1884. Moreover, the nonconformist movement had been essentially middle class and had hardly touched the workers of the towns. On the other hand, Disraeli's tradition and Chamberlain's influence were not enough to produce social legislation in sufficient quantity from the Unionist parties. The intellectualist movements represented by the Independent Labour party, the National Democratic Federation, and the Fabian Society were thus able to secure the collaboration of the trade unions, and the Labour party was born in 1899 and christened in 1906. Though not Marxist, it was definitely a "class" party, and it still relies mainly on working-class votes. Its base was broadened after 1920, however, and in any case it has never succeeded in obtaining the unanimous support of the working class.

Mr Lloyd George split the Liberal party not so much by replacing Mr Asquith in 1916 as by allowing the Conservative party managers to secure for their party a dominant position at the "coupon" election of 1918. The split weakened the party as a whole, while the Labour party by leaving the Coalition placed itself in a strong position to meet the inevitable reaction to the "khaki" election of 1918. For reasons mentioned in Chapter I, the electoral system established in 1918 further weakened the position of what had now become the "middle" party. Moreover, the decision of the Liberals to turn out the Conservatives and to support the Labour party in 1924, on the one hand made the Conservative party the real opponent of socialism, and on the other hand proved that the Labour party was the real alternative to Conservatism. The great Liberal effort of 1929 therefore failed, except in producing another Labour Government. The events of 1931 weakened the Labour party, but weakened the Liberal party still more. Putting up only 157 candidates in 1935, the latter could no longer claim to give the electors a middle path between Conservatism (as represented by the National Government) and socialism. The election of 1931 also had the effect of transferring from the Labour party much of the middle-class support that it had obtained between 1922 and 1929.

This rapid survey of history shows that the British parties do in fact represent different views of public policy. It is perhaps too much to dignify those opinions with the status of philosophies. <u>Primarily, they are reflections of different economic interes</u>ts. Those interests do not, however, prevent the existence of a very substantial "floating vote" which moves from side to side and thus determines, with the assistance of our electoral system, the results of elections. How large this floating vote is, nobody knows. Some say that it is a majority of the electors. Examination of the returns suggests, however, that it is not more than three million, and is probably less. In 1931 the Labour party can surely have obtained only the votes of the very faithful. It nevertheless obtained roughly 6,650,000 votes. In 1929, with few uncontested seats, it obtained about 8,390,000 votes and in 1935 it had 8,325,000 votes. Allowing for the fact that the pendulum had not quite swung over, that the Government vote had dropped, and that the electorate had increased, it is probably safe to assume a floating vote of 2,500,000 (which counts as 5,000,000 on a swing over) in an electorate of 31,000,000. Actually, a much smaller number is sufficient to give a majority, as a study of the constituencies shows.

A complete survey would occupy too much space. A study of electoral maps shows, however, the very uneven distribution of party support. The Conservatives always take Northern Ireland, except two seats in Fermanagh and Tyrone, which are represented by independents.

They also take most of the university constituencies. The rural constituencies are nearly all Conservative, except on the "Celtic fringe" of the North of Scotland, North and West Wales, and Cornwall, which are still Liberal.[1] In London, they take most of the wealthier suburbs as well as the City of London, Westminster, Holborn and Chelsea. Similarly, in the large towns the business centres (if large enough) and the residential suburbs are Conservative.

The Labour party usually holds the East End of London and the other working-class areas in the North-East and South-East of London. This Labour area extends to the boroughs to the East of London. Similarly, it usually holds the working-class sections of the large towns outside London, and smaller industrial towns like West Bromwich, Wednesbury, Stoke, Newcastle-under-Lyme, Ashton-under-Lyne, Wigan, Leigh, Rochdale, St Helens, Burnley, Nelson and Colne, most of the West Riding towns, South Shields, Morpeth, Rhondda, Merthyr Tydfil and Swansea. In the counties, it rarely holds many seats outside the industrial areas of South Wales, Durham, Staffordshire, Derbyshire, Nottinghamshire, Lancashire, the West Riding, Cumberland, and the Lowlands of Scotland.

This survey makes clear the "class" basis of the two parties. The great strength of the Conservative party lies in the commercial centres (where the "business premises" votes are conclusive), the wealthier residential areas, and the rural areas. The Labour party relies almost entirely on the working-class districts. Neither party can rely absolutely on the lower middle-class constituencies, inhabited mainly by clerks and other "white-collar workers". These lower middle-class constituencies really determine the result of the elections. In terms of London,

---

[1] And where, significantly, the middle class is still "chapel" and not "church".

for instance, the Conservatives are sure of the West End and the City, while the Labour party is sure of the East End. Whoever wins the inner fringe of northern and southern suburbs wins the election. In 1929 the Labour party managed (usually by pluralities in three-cornered contests) to take more of the mixed and lower middle-class areas. It also had a few rural constituencies, for instance in Norfolk. It is true to say, however, that the white-collar workers won the election. In 1931 the "doubtful" constituencies went Conservative, partly because there were fewer Liberal candidates to split the anti-Socialist vote, but above all because the white-collar workers were frightened back to Conservatism. In 1935, the relics of the nonconformist conscience, added to what has been called "the League of Nations vote", tended to go over to the Labour party. In addition, the activity of the Labour party on the London County Council had removed some of the suspicion that Labour members were "wild" and incapable.

This summary exposition is of course very simplified; but it is not too much to say that whoever wins the white-collar workers, or the lower middle-class constituencies, wins the election. If in every constituency where the National Government candidate was returned on a majority or a plurality of less than 6000 in 1935 (and most of them were lower middle-class constituencies) 3000 voters had transferred their vote to the Labour party, that party would just have had a majority in the House of Commons. The total number of votes required for this purpose was less than 750,000. It is therefore roughly true to say that in 1935 both parties were appealing for the support of 750,000 people, most of whom were white-collar workers.

This fact is as well known to Conservative party managers as it is to Labour party organisers. Of course, in appealing for a particular section of the voters, a party must not lose what it has already gained. The Conservative party must not lose the farmers' votes, because if the National Farmers Union put up its own candidates (as it has sometimes threatened to do when the Government does not take its agricultural policy from the Union) it is probable that the splitting of the Conservative vote would enable the Labour party to gain many of the rural seats. The Labour party has to be even more careful, because it has rivals on its other fringe, the Independent Labour party and the Communist party. If in the attempt to persuade the white-collar workers it becomes too respectable and reformist, it will tend to lose some of the voters who wear no collar at all and glory in their tieless state. Above all, it must never antagonise the trade unions, which provide most of the money and many of the votes. However, the trade unions, particularly the craft unions, are almost white-collar. It is possible to think of Mr Bevin in his shirt-sleeves, but it is a little difficult to imagine Sir Walter Citrine without a tie. The trade unions have fought too long for a high standard of living for them to believe with Moscow that they "have nothing to lose but their chains", and many of the white-collar workers are trade unionists. The bank clerks may be supercilious, but the railway clerks are not. Accordingly, the Labour party's path to power, if that is what matters, is through an extension of its support among the lower middle class.

This is not an argument but a fact. Some of the most brilliant speakers in the Labour movement are much farther to the "left", and they tend to assume that the divergence between the two parties is much greater than it is. The great weight of the trade unions, however, always comes down on the side of "moderation", and it is supported by the managers of "Transport House", who think in terms of votes. Consequently, though the constituencies prefer to listen to Sir Stafford Cripps or

Mr Harold Laski, those who dominate the decisions are the "moderates", whether they are politicians like Mr Attlee (of Haileybury and Oxford) or Mr Dalton (of Eton and King's), or are political organisers like Mr Herbert Morrison, or are trade-union organisers like Mr Bevin. It is not surprising, therefore, that there is far more in common between the two parties than is generally assumed. This assertion has already been made, and the reason is now clear. Both parties are trying to catch about 750,000 votes to be cast by the more prosperous workers (as in the Midlands) and the clerks and other white-collar workers in places like Hammersmith and Fulham. In order to show that this is indeed so, let us reduce the two programmes of 1935 to "slogans", and put them in parallel columns:

NATIONAL GOVERNMENT	LABOUR
Support the League of Nations.	Support the League of Nations.
Repair the gaps in our Defences.	Maintain adequate Defence Forces.
Disarmament.	Disarmament.
Increase Empire Trade. ⎱ Reduce Tariff Barriers. ⎰	Increase Trade by International Co-operation.
Insurance for Agricultural Workers.	Insurance for Agricultural Workers.
Support Agriculture and Fisheries.	Public Ownership of Land, and re-organisation of Agriculture.
Increase Home Trade. Maintain the Means Test but remove Hardships.	Abolish the Means Test and reduce Unemployment by Schemes of National Development.
Develop the Special Areas.	Vigorous Policy of National Planning for Special Areas.
Rationalise the Coal Industry. ⎫ Unify Mining Royalties. ⎬ Improve Safety in the Mines. ⎭	Public Ownership of Mines.
Improve Housing.	⎧ Healthy Homes at Reasonable Rents. ⎨ Abolition of "Tied" Cottages. ⎩ Cheap rural cottages.

NATIONAL GOVERNMENT	LABOUR
Contributory Pensions for Black-coated Workers.	Reduce age and increase amount of Old Age Pensions.
Reform of Education.	Big forward move in Education.
Improve Maternity Service. ⎫ Extend Child Welfare Service and Nursery Schools. ⎬	Vigorous Development of Health Services especially in relation to Maternal Mortality.
Deal with the Highlands and Islands.	Extend Mandate System for Colonies.
	Public Ownership of Banking, Transport, Electricity, Iron and Steel and Cotton.
	Comprehensive Programme of Industrial Legislation.
	Amend Trade Disputes Act.
	Repeal Penal Tax on Co-operative Societies.
	Abolish the House of Lords.
	Improve the Procedure of the House of Commons.

It will be seen that there are differences, especially at the end of the Labour list. Moreover, the use of slogans may hide the essential divergences. It was clear from the event, for instance, that "support the League of Nations" meant something very different to the National Government from what it meant to the Labour party. On the other hand, some of the differences are not so great as they appear. When the National Government promised to "unify mining royalties" it meant that the State should become owner of the royalties; and when it said that it would "rationalise the coal industry" it meant that it would leave the industry in the hands of private owners, but would impose large controls through a Coal Commission. On the other hand, when the Labour party demanded "public ownership" of the mines, it did not propose to confiscate the property of mineowners and royalty owners, but to vest it in a Coal Commission and compensate the owners. Again, the proposals at the end of the Labour list show an apparently wider divergence than there was in fact. The Treasury exercises wide hidden powers of control over the banks, and the effects of nationalisation would not be so great as might be supposed. Transport is already subject to wide powers of control under the Railways Act and through the powers of the Traffic Commissioners acting under general instructions from the Ministry of Transport. The generation of electricity was already subject to the wide powers of the Electricity Commissioners and the Central Electricity Board, and similar powers were already being considered for electricity distribution. The cotton industry was itself anxious for "rationalisation", and this involved, as the event proved, wide powers of control by (though not nationalisation under) a Cotton Commission. The abolition of the House of Lords may appear to be a fundamental change; but the House of Lords is of no importance under a National Government, and what the Labour party really proposed was that there should be either single-chamber government or an innocuous second chamber under a Labour Government as there is already under a National Government.

There are differences, and they are wide enough to give the elector a real choice. They are wide enough, also, to give rise to acute controversy in the House of Commons. The allegation is not that the two parties really have the same programme but that the question is one of more or less. They are differences of political theory and not mere differences of party. The elector's choice is not merely a choice of men but also a choice of measures. Nevertheless, there was much in the Labour programme with which a good Conservative might agree, and much in the programme of the National Government with which the Opposition could agree. It was much more an effort for Joseph Chamberlain to join the Unionist party than it would have been for Neville Chamberlain to have joined the Labour party. This is, of course, not a fair example, because Joseph Chamberlain was, on matters of social policy, to the left of the Liberal party, though it must be remembered that Neville Chamberlain was towards the right of the Conservative party. It is fair to say, however, that Mr Lees-Smith would have given up far less in joining the National Government than, say, John Bright gave up in opposing Gladstone. The Labour party's programme was that of socialist reformism; the National Government's programme was that of reformism without the adjective. There was no such fundamental opposition, as there was in the continental democracies, between the nationalist or capitalist parties and the Marxist parties. There could not be, so long as the two-party system operated; the two parties were offering bait to the same fish.

§ 3. *The Party Machines*

We have hitherto assumed that a party consists of a set of active politicians held together by common political principles. Until the middle of the nineteenth century such an assumption would have been almost accurate. In the eighteenth century a statesman in embryo did not "join a party", he merely looked round for a patron who owned or had "influence" in a borough or a county and was willing to secure the election of "a friend of Mr Pitt" or Mr Fox or Mr Canning. Even after the repeal of the Corn Laws in 1846 the Peelites were known as the friends or the followers of Sir Robert Peel. There is a relic still in the language of the House of Commons, where a member refers to another member of his own party as "my honourable friend" instead of "the honourable member".[1]

---

[1] Thus, in March 1940, Mr Hore Belisha was considered to have shown his disapproval of the Chamberlain Government by referring to the Prime Minister as "the right honourable gentleman" instead of "my right honourable friend".

The party was, in fact, a group of members in the House of Commons, together with the peers of the same political persuasion; or perhaps it would be more accurate to say that it consisted of the Whig or Tory lords together with their sympathisers and dependents and nominees in the House of Commons. After 1832, however, it was no longer possible to secure a majority by the nomination and influence of landlords and close corporations, and it therefore became necessary to elaborate an organisation in each constituency. Generally speaking, the initiative came from the constituencies or their members. Since the registration of electors depended primarily on private initiative, the essential function was to induce all political supporters to claim registration and to watch that the other party did not secure the registration of unqualified persons. The responsibility for registration is now vested primarily in the State, and this function is therefore no longer of importance, but the size of the local electorate compels the maintenance of an elaborate organisation for securing a candidate, conducting propaganda at all times (and more intensively during an election), and, above all, organising the election campaign itself. This local organisation is largely autonomous; but immediately after the second Reform Act in 1867 it was considered necessary for the Conservatives to make the most of the opportunity which they had gained through "dishing the Whigs", and a federation of local Conservative associations was formed. The body now known as the National Union of Conservative and Unionist Associations was thus established.

However, Disraeli's manœuvre did not succeed, and the Liberals captured most of the newly created working-class votes at the election of 1868. Accordingly, Disraeli decided that a more effective national organisation was required, and in 1870 he set up the Conservative Central

Office under his direct control, with a Party Manager appointed by him in immediate command. In 1872 it was arranged that the National Union should share offices with the Central Office, and that the two bodies should work in collaboration while retaining their separate organisations. Both conduct national propaganda, but the central funds are held by the Central Office and are thus under the control of the party leader.

The organisation of the Liberal party has sometimes led and sometimes followed that of the Conservative party. The Liberal Central Association, which compares with the Conservative Central Office, is however much more of a parliamentary secretariat, while the Liberal party organisation, which is based on the constituency parties, exercises many of the functions which in the Conservative party are exercised by the Central Office. In particular, it is the Organisation and not the Central Association which collects money for propaganda and assisting constituency associations. In other words, the funds of the Conservative party are under the direct control of the party leader; the funds of the Liberal party are under the control of the constituency associations.

The Labour party was founded by trade unions and socialist societies. It was only in 1918 that local Labour parties were formally established. Even now, the trade unions have larger representation in the National Executive Committee of the Labour party than the local Labour parties. There is, however, no leader and no "Central Office". The leader of the Parliamentary Labour party is elected by the members of Parliament every year, though he is usually re-elected. The chairman of the National Executive Committee changes from year to year. The statements of policy, which in the Conservative party are issued by the leader on his own responsibility, are issued by the National Council of Labour, which consists of the executive committees of the Labour party, the Parliamentary Labour party, and the Trade Union Congress. The secretariat in Transport House is under the control of the National Executive Committee, which is elected every year by the Annual Conference of the Labour party.

This short account gives a very incomplete picture of the complexity of organisation. No reference has been made to women's sections and youth organisations, bodies like the Primrose League, the Council of Action, and the Fabian Society, the societies of political agents, the educational activities of Ashridge, the Liberal Summer School, and the National Council of Labour Colleges, and a score of other matters which would need to be examined in order to give a complete picture of political organisation. It is clear from what has been said, however, that it is not easy to found a party to compete with an established party. The central activities of a party in a normal year cost something like £50,000. A general election costs another £25,000 or more—in grants to candidates fighting "forlorn hopes" and in propaganda. In addition each local association or party must find its own funds. In the Labour party and, in a few Conservative constituencies as well, these funds are obtained from small annual subscriptions. Most Conservative and Liberal candidates provide, however, at least a substantial part of the local funds. An ordinary election costs £500 if a great deal of voluntary labour and free committee rooms are available, or anything up to £1000 if they are not. Taking the country as a whole, a general election costs the Labour party between £300,000 and £350,000, nearly all of which comes from trade-union contributions, small local subscriptions, bazaars, whist drives, dances and such like. The Conservative party and its candidates probably spend an additional £100,000, though most of the total comes from the candidates.

It is not, however, merely a question of money. It has been shown by experience that even when the money is available an election in a constituency can be lost by the absence of "organisation". This means all kinds of things, the week-to-week conduct of propaganda (and not merely during the two weeks before the election, but consistently), a thorough canvass, the organisation of public meetings, the provision of transport for lazy, sick and aged voters, the checking of persons who have voted in order to find out who can still be persuaded to vote, and generally a consistent "drive" to urge the electors to the poll. It follows that few "independents" can stand for election with any hope of success, and people who dislike the existing parties find great difficulty in establishing a new one to suit them. These conclusions are important for the discussion which follows.

§ 4. *The Two-Party System*

In 1882 W. S. Gilbert thought it comical

> How nature always does contrive
> That every boy and every gal
>   That's born into this world alive
> Is either a little Liberal
>   Or else a little Conservative.

He was, of course, using his poetic licence to ignore the Irish Nationalist party. Apart from them, there have always been smaller parties and groups—Radicals, Peelites, Liberal Unionists, the Labour party, the Liberal party itself, Liberal Nationalists, National Labour members, the Co-operative party, the Independent Labour party, the Communist party. During the last hundred years, Governments without a party majority have been in office for twenty-eight years and Coalition Governments for twenty-nine years. Yet in substance Gilbert was right; there is a "natural" tendency for Great Britain to follow the two-party system. The Radicals merged into the Liberal party; the Peelites fused with the Whigs to form the Liberal party; the Liberal Unionists joined with the Conservative (and Unionist) party; the Labour party gradually displaced the Liberal party; and the Liberal Nationalists and the National Labour group would gradually have been absorbed into the Conservative party if there had been no war.

It is easy—too easy—to assert that the British peoples have a genius for compromise. It is better to say that they have learned to be tolerant. Cromwell saw that the country could not be governed if each insisted on enforcing his particular brand of truth, and Milton wrote a noble pamphlet in favour of the freedom of the press. As a whole, however, the Commonwealth men were as little tolerant as Laud, and it was by way of reaction to the rule of the "Saints" that opinion became reasonably free. Men became tired of religious controversy that led to civil war, and the existence of the papist King over the water compelled Protestants to make common cause. Whig leaders put latitudinarian bishops in control of the Church of England, and found it politically necessary to permit occasional conformity. When it ceased to be possible for the Scots to force the Solemn League and Covenant down English throats and the safety of the Hanoverian succession required union with Scotland, the English Parliament was prepared to guarantee the independence of the Presbyterian Church of Scotland and the Scottish Parliament to guarantee the predominance, in England, of the Episcopal Church of England. The nonconformists entered the period of "quietude" because, as a minority, they realised that their survival depended on their acceptance of toleration. "Private judgment" in matters of religion became the essential principle of the eighteenth century, so that it could reasonably be called "the age of reason". The national unity required for the conduct of the French wars was obtained by contrasting the liberty of Britain with the tyranny of France, and it came to be assumed that toleration was part of the Revolution Settlement. Apart from occasional "no-popery" riots, there was no serious religious oppression in the eighteenth century. The parties were still divided on religious issues; the Tories were the "Church party" and the Whigs had the support of the nonconformists. Nor could a party minister, until quite late in the eighteenth century, be sure that his fall would not be followed by his impeachment. After Culloden, however, the parties became dissociated from principles. A gentleman could be Whig or Tory according to his family connections, or to his prospects of political advantage if he was merely a careerist. Governments were made and destroyed by the adhesion and dissolution of groups until the French Revolution created a new party alignment. Fifty years before, Fox's strenuous opposition to Pitt's war would have led to impeachment or an Act of Attainder, but his "unpatriotic" action led only to removal from the Privy Council. Long before 1830, political opposition was as "respectable" as support of the King's Government.

After 1832, therefore, the Westminster battle became a debating match between rival parties angling for electoral support. The Peelites joined with the Whigs to form the Liberal party, and Disraeli nursed the dismayed Tories into the Conservative party. Because there were only two parties, with a few lone crusaders, each had to contain a wide variety of opinion. The Cavendish and the extreme radical both supported the Liberal party, and the die-hard and the Tory democrat both supported the Conservative party. In the classic age there was an oratorical duel between Gladstone and Disraeli (with the Irish butting in), but each had supporters who differed as widely among themselves as the leaders differed from each other.

Historical causes may account for the establishment of the two-party system, but they do not explain its continuance. There is a certain logic in the system. The policies which a Government can adopt are necessarily conditioned by the circumstances of the time. Free trade did not spring suddenly into the mind of Adam Smith and gradually win approval by the persuasiveness of its reason. It grew out of the economic conditions produced by the Industrial Revolution. Nor was the movement for social reform in the fields of factory conditions, public health, housing, pensions, social insurance and the like produced merely by the suggestions of benevolent publicists. Even Benthamism was the product of time and circumstance. The details of modern administrative law have depended on the accidents of personality and the chances of political predominance; yet it is not by imitation that all highly industrialised communities have followed much the same road. There is an inevitability about social movements that is obscured by the quarrels of puny politicians. For the most part, the real question has not been what policy shall be followed, but the speed at which the nation shall move towards an almost predestined end. Some wish to move rapidly and others more slowly. The cautious conservative has found his natural place in the Conservative party, and the more adventurous in the Liberal or the Labour party.

This, however, is an over-simplification. Parties do not represent only what may be called mental attitudes. They are essentially organs of interests. It has already been shown that since 1846 the two main parties have tended to represent different classes. The striking homogeneity of British economic life has in this respect played an extremely important part. The landed interest, the commercial interest, the shipping interest, the railway interest, the industrial interest, the industrial workers' interest, are with us valid generalisations because each has really been a unit. The smallness of Great Britain, the absence of internal restrictions upon the movement of capital and labour, and the unity of the home market, have prevented internal divisions. Moreover, none of them has been so distinct that there was any inducement for parties to split. As land decreased in importance, the "country party" claimed the support of other kinds of capital. As the workers gained the franchise, the employer and the salaried employee moved over with the *rentiers*. We have no peasants' party because we have no peasants. We have no agrarian party because the owners of land are also shareholders and company directors. We have no farmers' party because, in the main, the interests of landowners and farmers have been the same and, indeed, it would be impossible to distinguish the two classes.

Parties are not necessarily or entirely based on economic interests. In other respects the homogeneity of the population has assisted. The success of Protestantism prevented the Roman Catholics from becoming very numerous. Their minority status and the repressive legislation, only gradually relaxed, made it necessary that they should not engage in politics as Catholics, as they are apt to do where they are a strong minority. Religious differences have been important in the past; the Liberal party gave expression to the "Nonconformist Conscience" and the Conservative party supported the Church of England; but it has been explained that the doctrinal distinction was in large part an economic distinction as well. The Whig manufacturers were mostly dissenters, but their grandsons, the directors and *rentiers*, tended to join the Church. The Union with Scotland made the economic interests of the Lowlands paramount over Scottish nationalism, and once Prince Charlie went over the water for the last time, the Scots could forget that they were non-juring Tories and could vote for the Liberal party. The coal area of South Wales, too, was more coal than Wales.

The Irish were the exception, but an exception which proved the rule. Except in the north, they were different in history, religion and economic interest. In due course, therefore, the southern Irish formed their own party and thus upset the British Constitution by injecting a discordant element into the simple dichotomy which the electors and politicians of Great Britain found convenient for themselves.

We must not forget to add that, once the two-party system was firmly established in Great Britain, it was to the interest of party leaders to maintain it. Disraeli, more than any one, recognised that he must build his party and keep it under one roof. Even Lord Salisbury compromised with Lord Randolph Churchill until he could be sure that if he went he would go alone. Gladstone split the Liberal party, but only through a slight miscalculation; if John Bright had not decided against Home Rule, it is possible that Joseph Chamberlain might not have been so insistent on his private brand of Home Rule, and certain that few but the Whigs would have voted against the Home Rule Bill. Campbell-Bannerman performed Herculean feats to keep the two wings of the Liberal party together during the Boer War; and Balfour wrote strange economics and played even stranger politics to prevent Chamberlain from splitting another party.

Finally, we must remember that the Constitution itself was developed under the two-party system and does its best to compel it. It has been pointed out in Chapter I how the single-member system with straight voting favours the two main parties and operates against the "middle" party. The Labour party grew before 1914 because it appealed to a special economic interest which, it claimed successfully, was not adequately represented by the Liberal party. Its candidates could be successful in the industrial areas where that interest was dominant. The split in the Liberal party caused by Mr Lloyd George and the "coupon" election of 1918 gave the Labour party the opportunity to extend its influence in 1922, 1923 and 1924. The Liberals made a great effort in 1929 to recover the lost ground. They put up 512 candidates in order to make it plain to the electors that they were capable of securing a majority. Their $5\frac{1}{4}$ million votes, however, brought them 58 seats, while the $8\frac{1}{4}$ million Labour votes captured 287 seats. Had they held 145 seats, with the Labour party holding 249 and the Conservative party 256, as the votes were shared, it is probable that there would have been no split in 1932, that the party could have fought again in full force in 1935, and that the present position would be quite different. In fact, however, the single-member system went against them, and they had 16 seats only in 1935.

The electors have become so accustomed to the two-party system that an election is considered to be a choice of a Government. The question to be answered is whether or not the Government shall be replaced by the Opposition. Consequently, if a party is to receive much support, it must be capable of forming a Government. The great mass of the electors are not really interested in political principles, but they are concerned with what party obtains a majority. If it is true, as Conservatives have alleged since 1924, that their party is the "only alternative to socialism", then Liberals who dislike socialism will tend to vote Conservative; at the same time, the statement may be reversed; the Labour party is the only alternative to a Conservative Government, so that Liberals who dislike what they call "reaction" tend to vote Labour. The truth of these observations was demonstrated by the efforts made by the Liberal party to put up 500 candidates in 1929, and the insistence of its leaders that they were prepared to form a Government. The vote went against them, however, and in 1932 some Liberals preferred to give up free trade and continue in the National Government than to become a minor Opposition party again. In 1935 the Liberal party had only 157 candidates and received less than $1\frac{1}{2}$ million votes.

In the House of Commons, too, the third party has a difficult task, especially if it is a "middle" party. Modern parliamentary procedure assumes that nearly all proposals are made by the Government, and that the main debate takes place on a motion for rejection or amendment by the Opposition. The third party is thus constantly butting into what appears to be a private fight. It has to support either the Government or the Opposition, or else abstain from voting. If it supports one party constantly, it tends to be associated with that party in the electors' mind, and so he votes for or against that party. If it supports sometimes the one and sometimes the other, the elector thinks it inconsistent. If it abstains too frequently, it is said that it cannot make up its mind. And if, as usually happens, its members are to be found in both division lobbies, it is alleged not to be a party at all. Thus, the two-party system for this reason too tends to perpetuate itself. The Liberal party lost heavily in 1924 because it supported the Labour Government. By 1935, few electors understood where the party stood. It had supported the Labour Government in 1929–31, and the National Government until 1932. Then it had split and was appealing in two branches. The election returns suggest that most Liberal voters had murmured "confound your politics", and had abstained from voting.

Finally, the difficulty of establishing an organisation and of financing an election needs to be emphasised. In the main, this difficulty prevents rival parties being established. It also operates, however, to diminish the effectiveness of a declining party. The work is done in the constituencies by voluntary helpers. The prospect of victory, remote though it may be, is their reward. They will even go on fighting "forlorn hopes" provided that there is some chance of the party as a whole being successful. If the party seems doomed to perpetual minority status, however, their enthusiasm flags, and it becomes more difficult to fill committees. Again, candidates can be obtained only when there is some chance of obtaining a seat. This does not mean that candidates will not fight "forlorn hopes". Parliamentary candidature is almost a profession, and candidates expect to graduate from the forlorn hopes to the key constituencies, and perhaps from the key constituencies to the secure haven of a safe seat. A party cannot go on putting up 500 candidates of whom 450 will fail. Particularly is this true if the candidate has to provide a large part of the cost of the election. Yet a party that cannot put up 500 candidates at every general election is doomed to become a fragment. Again, the sums required for the central organisation cannot be obtained unless there is some chance that the party will form a Government. Rich men do not contribute money merely because they think that the "principles of Liberalism" or any other principles should be expounded. They expect to have the principles carried into practice even if they personally get nothing out of them. No party can manage on less than £50,000 a year, with another £25,000 in an election year; and sums of this order are not easily obtained by a minority party.

These are some of the reasons which have helped to establish and maintain the two-party system in this country. The question remains whether the system is desirable. A complete answer is impossible at this stage.

The British Constitution is a nicely balanced instrument, and a change anywhere produces a change everywhere. It will readily be admitted that two parties do not provide many of the combinations of policies which individual electors may require. In 1935, for instance, there were many who objected equally to the National Government's foreign policy and to the Labour party's domestic policy; and it is not surprising that a poll of only 74·4 per cent was recorded, the lowest since 1923. The more parties there are, the more electors find their needs met. Yet any system of election based on territorial constituencies becomes absurd with a multiplicity of small parties, even under a system of proportional representation, because so few first preferences count. Moreover, it is by no means so certain that the average elector is particularly interested in specific policies— except those which affect him personally, such as an increase in employment in his industry, or an increase in his old age pension. Even the intellectual, who knows exactly what he wants done, tends to vote on a party's general tendencies rather than on its specific proposals.

Further, the two-party system does provide stable government. There is a majority in the House of Commons and a Government responsible to that majority and controlling it. That Government is sure of having its measures passed (provided that it also controls the House of Lords); it can rely on its party majority so long as it does nothing directly contrary to its principles. It can act quickly and surely because it knows that it has the necessary backing. These are great advantages in a world troubled by ambitious dictators and difficult economic conditions. Minority governments are weak because they cannot govern. Coalition governments are generally weak because of internal dissension. In a world where strong and rapid government is necessary, only the two-party system works really well.

CHAPTER III

THE HOUSE OF
COMMONS

§ 1. *Political Ambition and its Rewards*

Greville tells us that when Lord Melbourne was invited to become Prime Minister, "he thought it a damned bore, and that he was in many minds what he should do —be Minister or no". His private secretary protested: "Why, damn it, such a position never was occupied by any Greek or Roman, and, if it only lasts two months, it is well worth while to have been Prime Minister of England." "By God, that's true," replied Melbourne, "I'll go." It lasted not two months but, with a short interval, seven years. Nor did Melbourne's action at the time of the "Bedchamber Plot" in 1839 suggest that he was anxious to leave. Naturally the post was more attractive than he had expected, since it fell to him to act as mentor to the young Queen. The story may not be true at all, but it is certainly true that "it is well worth while to have been Prime Minister of England".

Jokes are made about politicians in England as elsewhere; but the note of contempt and even detestation which is evident in some countries is noticeably absent. If it is something to be Prime Minister, it is also something to be a member of Parliament. There is a prestige attached to the House of Commons. It has a dignity which it rarely forgets. It is the focus of attention when stirring events are on foot, and the place to which the ordinary individual looks when he thinks that "something ought to be done" about his particular grievance. Political ambition not only is a virtue; it is commonly regarded as a virtue. A person does not soil his reputation by standing for election. It is not uncommon for individuals to choose a political career, not because money can be made out of it, but because "it is something to have been Prime Minister", or even to have been a plain member of Parliament.

Political activity does not lead to wealth. The salary of a member of Parliament is £600 a year, a small sum for a member who has to pay the expenses of his constituency organisation and of his election, and not a large sum even for a trade union official. The highest paid political posts are those of the Prime Minister and the Lord Chancellor, who receive £10,000 a year. The former has heavy expenses to bear and the latter is at the top of a profession which is extremely remunerative for the few who achieve leadership. There is nothing to be gained by company promoting, as Labouchere in one of his most cynical remarks suggested that there was. There is no "rake-off" from Government contracts, because members have no influence upon them. Occasionally it is alleged that the advocacy of a particular cause secures remuneration; but the private member's influence is so small that such opportunities must be rare and exceptional. In short, the most that can be obtained is the consciousness of a job well done, the admiration of a multitude, the power to make history, and a peerage to sweeten one's declining years.

These are, however, attractive prizes, and it is right that they should be so. The nation requires to devote the service of its ablest members to its own cause. The task of governing is too difficult to be undertaken by ignorant and vacillating minds. Western civilisation will be torn down by monomaniacs if the democratic States cannot rely upon the efforts of the most intelligent, the most farsighted, and the most altruistic of each generation. It is by no means certain that the British Constitution succeeds in this task. We must ask at a later stage what particular qualities are required of a statesman. It must be recognised, however, that for most the path to office must be through the House of Commons, and the system of election is not operated in such a way as to secure in that House a sufficient reservoir of talent.

For practical purposes attention needs to be concentrated on the Conservative and Labour parties, for it is from their ranks that Governments must generally be formed. The great difficulty of the Conservative party is that most candidates must be able to pay for their electoral organisation and their election expenses. It is therefore inevitable that the first question to be asked by a nominating committee is the amount which the candidate is able to pay. It is alleged that some constituencies demand as much as £3000 a year. If this is so, it may be taken to be exceptional. The salary of the secretary (who also acts as election agent), the wages of a typist, and the rent and other expenses of the premises, ought not to exceed together the sum of £1200 a year. Subscriptions to local charities, football, cricket and tennis clubs and the rest, may reach £1800 but can be very much less. The social activities—dinners, whist drives, "socials", dances, outings and the rest—ought to pay for themselves. In a well-organised constituency there will be some income from members. On the whole, it is probably correct to say that a person can secure a constituency capable of being won if he can afford £1500 a year and, say, £800 at every election. If he succeeds, he can set off the £600 a year salary, less income-tax.

These are, however, large sums. They imply that only

successful business men who can afford time for parliamentary duties, or successful professional men (such as lawyers, journalists, accountants, underwriters, stockbrokers) who work is mainly in London, or persons of "independent means", or the wives of any of them, can become Conservative members of Parliament. It does not follow that the ablest Conservatives of each generation are to be found in these classes. The bright young men and women who believe, rightly, that there is no career so desirable in a social sense as that of politics can occasionally find employment in the Conservative Central Office; but generally they must suppress their ambitions and first seek a living.

Moreover, the system gives to the Conservative party in Parliament a class bias far more emphatic than is warranted by its support in the country. The number of Etonians in the House is due not to the peculiar merits of Eton College but to the fact that it provides education for the sons of wealthy fathers. Nor is the number of retired officers of the Regular Army due to the political training given in Sandhurst and Woolwich. Still less is the number of company directors due to the special ability of members of the House of Commons or even —as is sometimes alleged—because "interests" want to have a "pull" in Parliament. It is said that Disraeli discovered the Conservative working-man: but it is easier for a camel to go through the eye of a needle than for a poor man to pass the Sergeant-at-Arms with a Conservative label to his coat-tails.

The Conservative party is aware of these difficulties, and from time to time they are submitted to examination. The only remedy is to achieve a large subscribing membership and, though this has been done in some constituencies, it is natural that the treasurers of "safe seats" should find it easier to secure a wealthy candidate than to go round with membership cards and a receipt book. It is, indeed, a fair generalisation that the safer the seat the wealthier the candidate. Wealth is not a disqualification for intelligence, but our social system does not provide that it shall be proportionate to ability.

The Labour party has a different problem. Few divisional Labour parties rely on securing a candidate who can pay organisation and election expenses. The party seeks to increase its paying membership, and the treasurer collects 1*d*. a week, or 1*s*. a quarter, from as many individuals as can be induced to subscribe. Funds are raised by social activities, bazaars, sales of work, and the rest. Special contributions are asked for to meet the expenses of elections. Moreover, local trade-union branches and co-operative societies make payments from their political funds. Also, many Labour members are content to live on £600 a year, and they are generally not expected to make large contributions to local charities. The sums required are smaller, partly because most of the work is done by voluntary labour, and partly because the divisional party does without premises unless it can afford them.

Nevertheless, a divisional party often has considerable difficulty in raising the funds required for a general election. If it receives an offer from a trade union to provide the funds, it rarely refuses, especially if the trade union has a large number of members in the constituency. In 1935, of the 552 Labour candidates, 118 were financed by trade unions; and of these 118 candidates, 77 were elected. In other words, less than one-quarter of the candidates were financed by trade unions, but exactly half the Labour members were. This shows —and more detailed examination proves the assumption correct—that the trade unions occupy many of the safest Labour seats. This would not matter if the unions exercised their choice wisely; but in fact they do nothing of the kind. They tend to appoint trade-union officials who are no longer wanted in their own organisation. Undoubtedly some of the Labour leaders, like Arthur Henderson, J. H. Thomas and J. R. Clynes, have been drawn from the union ranks, but the great majority have been "intellectuals". Of the seventeen former Labour ministers elected in 1935 (omitting the whips), only four were financed by trade unions, and of these only Mr Clynes was in the front rank.

§ 2. *The House and the Government*

The fact that the essential difficulty of the House of Commons is the paucity of governmental talent shows the relative importance of the functions of the House. We should not think of criticising the United States House of Representatives because it contained few if any prospective Presidents. It is not a nursery for administrators but a legislative body. Under the British system, however, the Prime Minister is almost invariably a member of the House of Commons, and the majority of the Cabinet is also drawn from that House. The Government exists because it has a majority in the House. It is a party Government whose strength is determined by its maximum vote when the whips are put on. It is for that reason that a general election is a choice of government. If it produces a Conservative majority, there will be a Conservative Government. If the party majority splits, there must be either a new Government or another general election.

The theory is that the House controls the Government. The Government, in the accepted phrase, is responsible to the House. In a very real sense the statement is accurate. It does not mean, however, that the House takes the proposals of the Government and moulds them according to its own wishes, as the French Chamber of Deputies did. Nor does it mean that the House gives instructions to the Government. It is equally true to say that the Government controls the House.

In normal circumstances the two-party system operates, and the Government has a homogeneous party majority. Sometimes the Government is a coalition and has to control two or three parties through their respective leaders. At other times, it has no majority, but has to collaborate with some other party—as Whigs collaborated with Peelites from 1846 to 1852, Conservatives with Liberal Unionists between 1886 and 1892, Liberals with the Labour party from 1910 to 1914 and the Labour Government with Liberals from 1929 to 1931. Where the support of another party is thus necessary, the leaders of that party, and not the House, control the Government. The fact is that the leaders of a party are reasonably certain of their followers: and where the members of the Government are the leaders the Government controls a majority of the House.

Implicit in this statement is the assumption that the party obeys the whip. It is extraordinarily rare for it to fail to do so. It is not so much that party discipline is strict. Even in the Labour party the appearance of strictness is greater than the reality. It is true that a recalcitrant member may find himself deprived of his "label" at the next election, and that it is the label which normally secures his return. In the Labour party, too, the label is presented by the National Executive Committee, by whom all "official" Labour candidates must be approved. This sanction is, however, rarely necessary. The apparent strictness of the Labour party is due to the fact that, while the party is in Opposition, its attitude towards matters before the House is determined by weekly meetings of the whole parliamentary party and not, as in the other parties, by the leaders sitting in the "Shadow Cabinet". A Labour member who dissents is thus opposing a majority, and

Parliamentary crisis:
Members arriving at the House

he is expected to do no more than abstain from voting.

The truth is, though, that a member of the Government's majority does not want to defeat the Government. Normally he is loyal to his leaders, and to vote against them is to break faith not only with them but also with his constituents, who elected him not because of his own opinions, nor because they thought that he was capable of exercising an independent judgment, but because he rendered allegiance to the party. They usually give him some latitude: but if he frequently votes against his own party he ought not to carry the party's label. The electors do not want men of independent views but good party men. They did not elect Sir Richard Roe but the Conservative candidate.

Moreover, it usually happens that the only way to vote against the Government is to vote with the Opposition. Frequently, the question is so framed that the member cannot conscientiously do so. For instance, if a Conservative Government introduces a Bill to subsidise the pigskin industry, the Labour Opposition will probably move an amendment stating that, since the only way to reduce unemployment in the industry is to bring it under public control, the House declines to pass the Bill. If the member believes that *laissez-faire* is the correct policy for the pigskin industry, he cannot vote in either lobby. Even if the question were so framed as to enable dissident Conservatives to vote against the Government, they would hesitate. The Government has in its hands (or strictly, the Prime Minister has) the power of dissolving Parliament. If it is defeated it may prefer to "appeal to the people" and not to "bow to the will of the House". The general election will cost members a substantial sum of money; some of them may be defeated; and possibly the Government will be defeated and the Labour party will come into power. Or the Government may not dissolve, but resign, and so bring in a Labour Government. As between the deep blue sea on this side and the devil on the other, the average member naturally prefers the deep blue sea, and his conscience is usually pliable enough not to insist that he throw himself overboard.

This argument applies to all parties, and it follows that a defeat of the Government with a majority is very rare. Strictly speaking, no majority Government has been overthrown by a party split since Robert Lowe led "the Cave of Adullam" against Gladstone's Reform Bill in 1866. There never was a majority for Home Rule in 1885, and there was no split in 1895 (when in fact, the Government had no majority). But, because the Government is normally sure of its votes, it can treat any vote as a "vote of confidence". The result is that (except on the rare occasions when the whips are not put on, or when a minority Government is in power) every vote is one of confidence. For an individual member to vote against the Government is thus to show lack of confidence in that Government. In other words, the question for the member is not whether he favours subsidies to pigskin manufacturers, but whether he supports the Government. The effect is cumulative. The majority votes for the Government, and therefore the Government controls the majority; because the Government controls the majority it insists on the votes of its majority. Cross-voting, except in minority parties, is rare.

This does not mean that the Government pays no attention to what is said in the House. It exists not because of the intelligence of its members or the excellence of its intentions, but because it won a majority at the last election. It will continue to exist only if it secures a majority at the next election. It will secure a majority only if its followers secure majorities or

pluralities in their constituencies. Members must therefore sniff every breeze that blows, lest it develop into
a gale that sweeps away enough votes to lose their seats.
If any act of the Government threatens to lose votes, they
will not vote against the Government in the lobbies but
will complain to the whips in the smoking-room. A
strong Government will resist pressure if it thinks that,
ultimately, it can put its case and win: but the strongest
Governments bow to the inevitable by gracefully
acceding to the "sense of the House". It is because of
this, as has already been emphasised, that we have
Government by the people.

Nor is this all. Not all Government supporters are
pliant yes-men. They will not be beaten with whips and
they wage war on ministerial scorpions. The House can
be driven, but is far more easily led. A carrot may move
a donkey when a dozen whips will not; and, after all,
members of Parliament are sometimes quite intelligent
donkeys. A way out must be managed, and management
is often nothing more than an ability to make concessions gracefully.

It must be remembered, too, that members are not
mere representatives of their constituents. The association of Labour members with trade unions and co-
operative societies has already been mentioned. The
close connection between other members and other
bodies known generally in America as "pressure groups"
is less well understood. When the Labour Government
consulted the Trade Union Congress, its opponents
spoke of "outside dictation"; but the language of
opposition must not be adopted too easily. The connection between the Conservative party and the Drink
Trade is perhaps less close than it was before 1914,
because "the Trade" has never recovered from the
combination of Mr Lloyd George's restrictions and the
attractions of Hollywood; high prices and sex appeal

have driven men from drink, and though the public-house has lost no profits its political influence has declined. Besides, women now have votes. There are, however, hosts of pressure groups, of which the National Farmers' Union and the Mining Association have been the most successful. In our Constitution these groups seek to act upon the Government because privileges come from the Government even if they pass by way of the House. It is wise, however, to provide for bringing up reserves, and most pressure groups have representatives in the House. Nor need they be in one party only. Where extra profits are sought they must necessarily be obtained through parties that do not treat profit as sin; but where what is wanted are better conditions for public employees, better social services, or "justice" for little men, it is better to secure representation in all parties.

Consequently, the member for Casterbridge may also be member for the National Union of Pigskin Manufacturers or the National Association of Public Stenographers. When a question affecting his second constituency is before the House, he is provided with a brief which needs only a few "Mr Speaker"'s to become an eloquent speech. He states publicly what has already been urged upon the minister privately. If a concession will gain a few votes, or if administration will become easier if the goodwill of the association is obtained, or if the request for "justice" is not ill-founded, the minister will concede gracefully in the House what he has already accepted outside. Indeed, the honourable member's speech may bring to the minister's attention an argument which hitherto had stopped much lower in the official hierarchy. In any case, the glory will go to the honourable member, who will naturally receive the gratitude and applause of the association at its next annual dinner.

It must not be forgotten, though, that the last word

as well as the first rests with the Government. The major legislation enacted by Parliament is the Government's legislation. The foreign and imperial policy of the nation is the Government's policy. Taxation is imposed by Parliament but determined by the Chancellor of the Exchequer. The Government not only proposes but, through its majority, disposes. Even so, it is not the Government standing alone. It is the Government in Parliament. It is a Government, too, whose only authority is the support of public opinion witnessed for the time being by its majority in the House of Commons. Its policy must in the near future be submitted to the people. The axe will fall upon those who lose touch with public opinion: and the longer the blow is parried the more heavily it will fall—as the Conservatives discovered in 1906.

It cannot be said that this is dictatorship. At worst it is dictatorship for a term of years certain; but dictators who at short intervals have to beg the people for votes freely cast are the servants of the public and not its masters. Those who regret the snows of yester year do not realise that yester year was long ago when the great landowners governed *en société anonyme*; and the snows were an intolerable nuisance. Government is too complicated a business to be conducted by 615 persons in open debate. It requires the whole apparatus of study and execution which is described in Chapter VI. Behind every proposal is a great collection of files, a long series of committee meetings, a large number of individual discussions and, indeed, the whole mechanism of administration. Parliament cannot govern. It can do no more than criticise. Moreover, we have discussed these questions in terms of the majority. Facing the Government Front Bench is the Opposition Front Bench. There is no dictatorship so long as there is an Opposition.

§ 3. *The Opposition*

If Parliament's main function is to criticise, the Opposition is its most important part. Its members are, so to speak, critics by profession. It has often been pointed out that the House of Commons, unlike most other legislatures, has its seats arranged not in a semi-circle, but facing each other in two large blocks separated by a gangway. To the right of the Speaker are the Government and its supporters: to the left is the Opposition. There is no gradation from right to left, but a clear division. A member who gradually loses faith in the Government cannot proceed by easy stages; he must wait until he is ready to take the great decision to "cross the floor". It is true that there are more subtle distinctions. A minister who resigns because he disagrees with the Government's policy speaks from a seat "below the gangway" which separates the Treasury bench from the benches farther away from the Speaker. The leader of a minority party similarly speaks from "below the gangway" on the Opposition side. Fundamentally, however, the topography of the House recognises the stark division of the two-party system.

The members of the Government sit on the front bench to the right of the Speaker and the leaders of the Opposition on the front bench to his left. Opposite the Cabinet, therefore, is the "Shadow Cabinet" (though it is not so called in the Labour party): opposite His Majesty's Government is His Majesty's Opposition. It is a strange name, first used in jest; yet it is so expressive that it has become almost official. The Opposition is His Majesty's alternative Government: only a small change in voting at the next election is necessary to compel Government and Opposition to change places. The Leader of the Opposition even has a salary, charged on public funds, so that he may exercise his public functions without the distraction of earning a living.

This fact shows more plainly than anything else that opposition is regarded as an essential part of the Constitution. It proves how unjust is the charge of dictatorship. The British Constitution not only does not expect conformity, it demands the opposite. The Government has its majority and so can govern; but it must do so under a constant fire of criticism from the Opposition. Opinion outside is assumed to be divided; therefore it is desirable that inside the House ministers may be reminded of Cromwell's injunction: "I beseech you, in the bowels of Christ, think it possible that you may be mistaken." Nor can ministers forget that politically they are mortal. What the Opposition says may be so persuasive that the "floating vote" may "swing the pendulum". Ministers must answer argument by argument; they must meet a half-truth by a whole truth (or a more attractive half-truth) lest it run round the country. In this way the appeal to the people is not an occasional ceremony, but a process which goes on daily and hourly in the parliamentary session.

No doubt opposition delays the process of government. Between 1 and 7 September 1939 Parliament passed enough legislation to occupy two or three sessions, because the Opposition agreed not to oppose. In wartime a Government expects and receives power to legislate by Order in Council because enemies do not travel at the speed of the democratic process. It must be remembered, however, that we demand not only action but just action—action that is subjected to public approval or disapproval. Nor is the delay so great as might appear, because the administrative process also is long, and it is prepared while legislation is in Parliament.

Frequently, too, debate embarrasses the Government. How easy it would have been for the Chamberlain

Government to have ridden off after Trondheim if it had not to meet the criticism which inevitably followed! Negotiations with foreign powers are difficult to conduct when a lynx-eyed Opposition sits suspiciously on the watch. We might have a better foreign policy if we had no Parliament: but we might have a worse; and what is better and what worse is generally a matter of opinion. We are a free people because we can criticise freely and, if our criticisms prove persuasive, compel the Government to withdraw. Public opinion has destroyed a good many Bills and has reversed a good many policies. The spear-head of the attack is the Opposition. To find out whether a people is free it is necessary only to ask if there is an Opposition and, if there is, to ask where it is.

All this assumes, of course, that the House debates in public. Government and Opposition speak to each other, but for the education of the people. The criticisms brought against the Government are the criticisms of ordinary individuals; the answers of the Government are formally answers to the Opposition, but substantially they are replies to the questions raised in the factory, the railway carriage and the office. The members of the House of Commons were not elected for their special qualifications, but because they supported the policies which the majority of their constituents were prepared to accept. They have no authority except as representatives, and in order that their representative character may be preserved they must debate in public. Secret sessions were suited to the oligarchic government of the eighteenth century. They are the negation of democratic principles. No doubt there are exceptional occasions when secrecy is justified. Compulsory military service was until recently contrary to the British tradition. In 1916 it was considered necessary in the interest of the community to propose compulsory enlistment. In normal times a change so great could not be effected without a "mandate" from the people obtained by including the proposal in a party manifesto at a general election. In 1916 it was impossible to have a general election. What is more, it was impossible, without giving information of great value to the enemy, even to explain the reasons fully in public. On the other hand, no Government can be trusted to make so great a change without detailed explanation. It was therefore necessary that the explanation should be made in a secret session. The procedure was justified by the exceptional conditions. No such conditions arose during the first year of the present war. Naturally, the Government must not give information which might be useful to the enemy; but this means only some extension of the discretion which is always accorded to a Government. So long as the general direction is clear and approved, there is no need for the Government to give detailed explanations. The only great change of policy in the present war was produced by the resignation of the Chamberlain Government, and this was brought about by a public debate. Nevertheless, there have been six secret sessions during the first year of war. Not one of these was justified by the conditions. Information which cannot be given publicly need not be given privately. Indeed, on the last occasion, on 30 July 1940, it was not even suggested that additional information might be given. The debate was an ordinary debate on foreign affairs in conditions not essentially different from those in which many debates have been held since 1936. A secret session was chosen by a majority on a free vote merely because members did not want to tie their tongues with discretion. This is the negation of the principles of representative government, and it is no more justified in war than it is in peace. In fact, the attitude of members was based on a complete misunderstanding of their authority. They appeared to think that, as members, they had something particular to contribute to the conduct of the war, that their views on military strategy or foreign policy were of more value than those of Tom, Dick or Harry. The truth is that they are Tom, Dick and Harry. They were not elected to contribute special knowledge or special ability to the conduct of affairs; they were chosen because they were ordinary people capable of representing ordinary people. Their functions, as Mr Greenwood correctly stated at the outbreak of war, are to bring the views of ordinary people to the attention of the Government and to act as channels through which explanations can be given to ordinary people by the Government. They are representatives only, and they can be representatives only in public. The present House differs from an ordinary House only in that there is now no Opposition. The tasks which the Opposition normally fulfils must now be undertaken by private members.

Even in normal times, it is not the business of an Opposition to obstruct government. Its purpose is to criticise, not to hinder. There are no doubt exceptional circumstances where obstruction is permissible. Given the assumptions of the Irish Nationalist party, no blame for obstruction can properly be laid against them. Their concern was not to make the Union workable but to destroy it. Moreover, where a Government is forcing a policy on the country which it is reasonably certain that the country does not approve, the Opposition may reasonably demand that it be submitted to the people. It is not so easy to interpret this principle. The Government naturally reads the signs one way and the Opposition another. For instance, the Conservative Opposition obstructed the Parliament Bill in 1911 and Home Rule in 1912. The Liberal Government had a majority after 1910 only with Labour and Irish support. The Conservatives therefore said that the Liberals had a mandate for neither, because the Irish voted for the Parliament

Bill to secure Home Rule, and Great Britain had produced a majority against both. Whether the "predominant partner" alone had a right to determine the course is a question which must be left to the reader. It should be said, however, that a party which proposes to use its majority while in power should accept a majority verdict against it. Obstruction brings parliamentary government into contempt, and it is both politically wise and constitutionally sound not to overemphasise lawyers' arguments about "mandates". If a Government offends public opinion by a too extensive use of its power, the Opposition will reap the benefit.

However, remedies have been devised to meet obstruction. It is no longer possible to "talk out" a proposal by lengthy speeches and much repetition. When the Speaker considers that enough has been said, the Government (or any member) can move that "the question be now put" and so use its majority to closure the debate. A multiplicity of amendments can no longer be moved because the Speaker or Chairman has power to "select" those which appear to raise the essential issues—a power known as the "kangaroo". Finally, if it appears that the debate on a Bill will be long, the Government can always move a "guillotine" resolution to closure the debate by compartments—to allot, that is, so many hours to the discussion on each stage and each group of sections.

These devices add to the power which the Government possesses by virtue of its majority. Indeed, the closure and the guillotine can be used only where the majority obeys the whip. Great though the power is, the Government recognises the right and the duty of the minority to criticise. It must do so, for an attempt to "gag" could be represented as arising from a recognition of administrative failure and would be a powerful argument in favour of the Opposition. It is therefore natural that parliamentary proceedings should in the main be regulated by what are politely called "the usual channels" which are said to pass "behind the Speaker's Chair"—in other words, by negotiations between the two or three sets of whips.

Private members are allowed to move motions on about twelve Wednesdays and to debate Bills introduced by them on about eighteen Fridays (when the sittings are short) during the session. Even here the whips are not without influence, because often private members (who have to draw lots for the opportunity) are called upon suddenly to produce Bills and motions, and if their powers of rapid invention of grievances are not good, it is natural for them to seek the advice of the whips. In fact, while the Labour party is in Opposition, the party meeting itself determines what subjects shall be raised by Labour members who are successful in the ballot. On the Government side members sometimes produce their own ideas, and sometimes ideas elaborated by pressure groups; but often a motion or a Bill comes not from the private member's head but from the whips' pigeon-holes.

This is, however, a very small proportion of the business of the House; and the rest of the time is taken up by Government business. The time covers, in fact, three full days a week up to about Easter, four full days up to about Whitsuntide, and the whole week of five days thereafter. Also, it needs only a majority vote, proposed by the Government, to deprive private members of their time altogether (as in the session 1939–40). It is the Government business which is arranged with the Opposition. Every Thursday the Leader of the Opposition asks the Prime Minister what is the business for the coming week. He knows the answer already, because the two of them have arranged it through the whips: but this is a convenient method of informing the

House. The Government has a rough plan for the
session, arranged by the Home Affairs Committee of
the Cabinet. It brings up the business in the order convenient to itself; but there is a good deal of leeway.
There are, for instance, twenty "Supply days" for
debating Estimates. It does not matter in what order
they are taken. If the Opposition wishes to attack the
Government's foreign policy, the Chief Whip offers to
have the Foreign Office vote put down for Tuesday,
provided that the Opposition will allow the Committee
stage of the Pigskin Industry (Reorganisation) Bill to
be completed on Monday. It is so agreed, and on
Tuesday the Foreign Secretary moves the Foreign Office
vote and puts the Government's case. The "Shadow
Minister" for Foreign Affairs on the Opposition side
then attacks the Government and perhaps moves to
reduce the vote by £100 because of the dangerous and
vacillating policy of the Government. The debate ebbs
and flows across the gangway until, at about 9.30 p.m.,
another front-bench speaker on the Labour side "catches
the Chairman's eye". It happens that about 10.15 p.m.
the Under-Secretary for Foreign Affairs catches the
Chairman's eye and, strange to relate, he runs out of
arguments just before 11 o'clock, when the House must
adjourn, and it appears that no other member wishes
to speak. The Opposition amendment is put to the vote
and is, of course, lost. Probably, the Foreign Secretary
will now ask leave to withdraw his motion, because the
Opposition may want to attack the Government's
foreign policy on another day. The surprising order-
liness of this procedure is not surprising at all, because
it was all arranged by the whips beforehand.

Nor is this an isolated example. It is part of the
ordinary procedure. When this is made clear, some
people denounce the whole thing as a sham, especially
if they regard the Government as the tools and the

Opposition as the dupes of some mysterious, nefarious and most able people known as "the Capitalists"— preferably with an unprintable adjective. It is nothing of the kind. It is an exhibition of the logic of the democratic system. The Government must govern and the Opposition must oppose; what is more desirable than that they should arrange for their functions to be exercised in the best and most orderly fashion? The Government has power to obstruct opposition, and the Opposition has power to obstruct government: but neither kind of obstruction is desirable. Confusion will result if both make the attempt; and if one of them does, it will get a black mark in many an elector's register. It is particularly necessary for the Labour party to be "constitutional", because the floating vote consists of a good many people who can be frightened into voting Conservative by a mere suggestion that the fundamentals of the British Constitution are being tampered with. Besides, the Labour party has a respect for the power of the majority (as its own "discipline" shows) which has never afflicted Conservatives like the late Lord Birkenhead or the late Lord Carson, not to mention living persons. Indeed, the accusation made by the Conservative press as well as by some sections of the Labour movement was that the Parliamentary Labour party under Mr Attlee's leadership was not effective enough— was, in other words, altogether too constitutional and gentlemanly.

The efficiency of this system of government by crosstalk depends on the ability of the House to find able and acceptable chairmen. Nothing exhibits so well the genius of the British Constitution or, more accurately, the reasonableness of British people, as the position occupied by Mr Speaker. He is chosen by the Government from the Government benches when there is a vacancy. Invariably, however, the Opposition is consulted, and its veto is conclusive. He is intended to be as impartial as any human being can be. Accordingly, he must be chosen from among those members who have not made themselves conspicuous by the virulence of their politics. Often he has served a long apprenticeship as Chairman or deputy Chairman of Ways and Means, so that he may for many years have presided over the House in committee, or over the House itself during the Speaker's absence. Before that he may have been one of the members of the Chairmen's panel, selected by the Speaker from all parties to preside over Standing Committees and to act as temporary Chairman of the House when occasion arises. It is by no means uncommon for a Standing Committee with a Government majority to be presided over by a member of the Opposition. In the exercise of his functions he does not hesitate to overrule a minister or his own leader. Nor does the minister or leader hesitate to accept the ruling. The House has long ago realised that it can do nothing unless it has good chairmen. It has, therefore, deliberately exalted their status. A member of the Chairmen's panel and a Chairman of Ways and Means share in the great prestige of the Speaker.

That prestige is maintained with all the art which the British Constitution knows so well how to employ. Outside Parliament, Mr Speaker is for ceremonial purposes the House of Commons. His election is rarely opposed in his constituency. Inside the precincts but outside the Chamber forms and ceremonies support his dignity. He is preceded by the Sergeant-at-Arms carrying the succession of "that bauble" which Cromwell ordered to be removed. His procession moves through the corridors to the call of "Speaker", and in the central lobby his coming is notified by the command "Hats off, strangers!" Standing at the bar of the House of Lords it is he who acts as "House of Commons" when the King or his Commissioners sit "in Parliament". Inside the House his word is law. His rising is a signal for the member "on the floor" to sit. He insists that he, and not other members, be addressed. He requires that members do not cross between him and the member speaking. Members bow to him as they leave the Chamber. The importance of these apparently empty ceremonies must be emphasised because, though they often make ardent reformers impatient, they really have a purpose. It is natural and pardonable that a new member straight from the Clyde should despise this "mummery", which appears to him to be intended to prevent him from discussing fully and adequately the empty stomachs, the lice, the leaking roofs, and the rest, that induced him to become a politician. It is, however, part of the process of enabling that member to put his case. Other members dispute the causes and may deny the facts. Debates on subjects on which political passion runs high is possible only if it is conducted with dignity and decorum. Reforms cannot be carried in a beargarden, nor is logical argument effective in its popular appeal if it is conducted in a monkey-house. The ceremonies which attend Mr Speaker assist in creating that "atmosphere" which is so potent in making the parliamentary system workable. Order is the primary requisite of freedom.

It must not be assumed that parliamentary procedure represents the highest degree of wisdom. It is always undergoing development, but here as elsewhere reforms are apt to come tardily. A discussion of present difficulties would involve an examination of rules and practices of a technical order which would be out of place in this book.[1] It may be said, however, that the

---

[1] See Jennings, *Parliament* (Cambridge University Press, 1939) for a description of the technique; and Jennings, *Parliamentary Reform* (Gollancz, 1933) for some possible remedies.

problem lies in the apparent contradiction between two demands, for speed on the one hand and full and comprehensive discussion on the other hand. The solution involves a distinction between general principles and technical details. The former only are suitable for discussions on the floor of the House in these days, while the latter must be left to smaller committees "upstairs". At present a vast amount of detail is examined by a thin House in the Chamber itself, with the result that the parliamentary process is slower than it need be, and parliamentary debate less effective in its popular appeal. It has, too, the further result that technical devices, especially in the realm of finance, are adopted to limit the scope of general debate lest, in ranging widely, it take up more time. The rule which, in substance, prevents a member from proposing an increase of expenditure, dates in its present rigour only from 1919. Its foundation was laid in the eighteenth century, when the fear was strong that members might curry favour with the monarch by offering him more revenue. It is now defended on the ground that it prevents that "distribution of the pork-barrel" which arises where members in other legislatures support each other's demand for expenditure in their own constituencies. Such a restriction is, however, unnecessary where a Government controls a majority and the Chancellor of the Exchequer sits on the "pork-barrel". The real reason for the maintenance of the rule, and for its growing rigidity, is that it limits debate on Government proposals and so enables them to be passed more quickly. In other words, the demand for speed overrides the demand for wide discussion. It is not impossible to achieve both, but only by a series of minor technical reforms which have hitherto met with opposition.

CHAPTER IV

THE HOUSE OF LORDS

§ 1. *A Conservative Bulwark*

The House of Lords shares with the Corporation of the City of London the privilege of having passed almost unscathed through the "reform" movement which began about 1782 and developed with great vigour after 1830. The reason is not that there has been universal satisfaction with its work. Indeed, dissatisfaction has gradually extended to all parties. There is now agreement that changes are necessary; but the problem as to what these changes shall be lies right at the centre of political controversy. The House of Lords is for practical purposes an outpost of the Conservative party, though the peers possess a greater freedom of action than the Conservative members in the House of Commons. Changes made under a Conservative Government are hardly likely to prove acceptable to its successors, and changes could not be made under any other Government without a controversy between the two Houses.

The Conservative party has an immense majority because, subject to all the qualifications which have already been set out, the division between the parties is in essence a class division and the peers are drawn from one class only. Indeed, the gradual "Conservatisation" of the House is one of the means of showing that the party division is, in large measure, an economic division. So long as Whigs disputed with Tories, the party strength among the peers depended primarily on which party had been longest in office. In 1712 the Whigs had a majority, and the Tory Government created twelve new peerages in order to pass the Treaty of Utrecht. In 1832 the long period of Tory government—practically from 1784 to 1830—gave the Tories a majority of about fifty. The Whigs were in office from 1830 to 1841, and from 1846 (with two short intervals) until 1866. About 1865 the two parties were fairly evenly balanced. At least since 1832 there had been a tendency for traditionally Whig families to become Conservative, because the Liberal party was the party of reform, the party whose strength lay among dissenting manufacturers and not among Anglican landowners. The tendency was offset by the creation of new peerages under Liberal Governments. However, the association of liberalism and radicalism under Gladstone after the second Reform Act caused the movement to become much more rapid. In 1886 the Whigs parted company with the Liberals over Home Rule: only forty-one peers voted for the second Home Rule Bill in 1893. In 1911 it would have been necessary to create five hundred peers to secure the passage of the Parliament Bill. The rise of the Labour party completed the process. Of the 746 members of the House in 1936, 543 indicated their support of the National Government, 56 were Liberal, and 16 Labour. The others stated that they were "independent" or gave no information. In order to make certain of passing a measure, a Labour Government would thus require some 750 Labour peers.

Whatever their political opinions, however, peers are responsible to nobody save themselves. Whether of the first or the fourteenth generation they take their seats by their own right, except that the sixteen Scottish representative peers have to secure re-election at the beginning of every Parliament by the thirty or forty members of their own order. They need no labels. They take the whip because they desire it, not because they require it. No jealous constituency watches their votes, or notes how assiduously they attend to their duties. They have not to trim their sails to the breezes of public opinion. They can decide as their reason or their private interest indicates. Consequently, Conservative peers are usually more conservative than the Conservative party. They come from a narrow section of society, that section usually printed as Society. They have not, as the Conservative party has, to prove to working-class and lower middle-class people that Conservatism is the best policy for all classes. In the party sense they need not be good Conservatives.

Nevertheless, a Conservative Government is always quite certain of its majority. It may have to grant concessions in the House of Lords as in the House of Commons. It must not antagonise the landowners, or the coalowners, or the whisky interest. They are, after all, representative of important political groups, and some of them probably contribute substantially to party funds. This is, however, a question of "management" differing not fundamentally from that in the House of Commons. No Bill promoted by a Conservative Government has been rejected by the House of Lords since 1832; and, for the last fifty years at least, no Conservative Bill has been amended against firm Government opposition.

The position of other Governments is quite different. Not many peers attend—rarely more than two hundred, and usually not more than eighty—but among them is always a Conservative majority. This majority usually obeys the commands of its leaders, though sometimes it defeats the Government when its leaders suggest that

The Lords mutilate the Ballot Bill, 1872

it should not. The leaders themselves determine their strategy in consultation with the Conservative leaders in the House of Commons. Nothing passes the House of Lords except by permission of the Conservative party, whether that party is in office or in opposition.

This does not mean that no Liberal or Labour legislation passes the House of Lords. For the Conservative peers to adopt such tactics would be to invite the destruction of their privileges. They must exercise their power according to some principle which can be defended by Conservative politicians in the country. They exercise what Lord John Russell in 1839 called "a wise discretion" and claim to reject legislation only when it does not appear clearly that it has the support of the country. Even if this principle were honestly applied, it would assume that Conservative peers, who never fight an election, are better judges of public opinion than those who have to persuade a majority of the electors to support them at intervals. In practice, however, the principle is a mere excuse. To suggest that the Education Bill of 1902 was passed because it was supported by the country, while that of 1906 was amended out of existence because it had not the support of the country, is just nonsense. The country had little to do with it. The real reason was a combination of honest opinion and party tactics; and, be it remembered, the alleged principle does not allow rejection or radical amendment even on grounds of opinion—it is public opinion and not the peers' opinion which is used to justify their action. The House naturally passes Bills of which it does not disapprove. It passes other Bills if it is tactically wise to do so. It radically amends if it considers that the Government would prefer a mutilated Bill to no Bill at all, or if it is tactically less dangerous to amend than to reject. It rejects if the Conservative party is prepared to risk an election, or if it is believed

that the Government will acquiesce without a dissolution.

Lord Balfour one said, while he was leader of the
Unionist party, that it was the bounden duty of his
audience to see that "the great Unionist party should
still control, whether in power or whether in Opposition,
the destinies of this great Empire". Such a claim could
not be justified. It is, however, possible honestly to
support the Conservative claim to halt measures of a
radical nature until the "mind of the country" has been
made up. Though most Conservatives agree that the
House of Lords needs reform, they do not accept the
argument that it needs reform because it is Conservative.
Every Conservative plan of reform so far put forward
would give a Conservative majority. Nor are they
necessarily thinking of party advantage. In their view,
the Liberal and Labour parties often advocate rash and
immature plans of social reform which, if carried out,
would be dangerous to the peace and economic stability
of the British Empire. Such plans may be superficially
attractive to the electorate, particularly if they are
accompanied by wild promises of future benefit. They
may be sprung suddenly on the electorate at a general
election; or they may be so wrapped up in a multitude
of proposals that their significance may not be plain.
They may even be carried through the House of Commons without having been part of an election programme. Further, a Government with a majority in the
House of Commons has not necessarily a majority in the
country. It may never have had such a majority, or it
may have lost it long before the Parliament comes to
an end. Finally, a majority for a Government is not
necessarily a majority for every specific proposal made
by the Government.

Some of these arguments apply to a Conservative
Government as to a Labour or Liberal Government.

A Conservative Government does not, however, propose
"rash" or "revolutionary" or "radical" measures.
Consequently, a Labour or Liberal Government requires
a Conservative brake, while a Conservative Government
is, so to speak, a slow-moving vehicle which is never
likely to get out of control. Hence, it is argued, a Conservative majority in the Second Chamber is very desirable, so long as it exercises its powers reasonably, as
most Conservatives allege that it has done for the past
century. The only reform required is in the composition
of the majority, and most Conservative schemes of reform
provide for a substantial reduction in the number of
hereditary peers sitting in the House and for the addition
of new "Lords of Parliament" elected by the House of
Commons or by local authorities.

It will be seen that some of the arguments could be
met by a more accurate system of political representation in the House of Commons, though it was Conservative members who defeated such proposals in 1918
when the peers supported them, and the Conservative
party has always refused to adopt them. Other arguments depend upon a fundamental suspicion of democracy based on a wide franchise. Moreover, the whole
assumes that a Conservative majority will always act
reasonably. There is very little basis for such an assumption. Sweet reasonableness is no more a Conservative
characteristic than it is a Labour or Liberal characteristic.
All power is likely to be abused unless it is adequately
checked. The power of the House of Commons is
checked by the ultimate power of the electorate. Sharp
practices of the kind which Conservatives fear reap their
reward at the next election, as was discovered by the
Conservatives after the "khaki" election of 1900, by
Mr Lloyd George after the "Hang the Kaiser" election
of 1918, and by the Conservatives after the "Red
letter" election of 1924. The reward is not garnered until

the next election, but in the meantime the seeping away of its support is evident to the Government. It is a complete fallacy to assume that, because a government has a majority in the House of Commons it can do what it pleases. Though every Parliament passes laws which would not be accepted by the electorate as separate proposals, the Government's general tendency must be in accord with public opinion lest it be thrown out of office for a decade. Nor is there any cause to fear the electorate. The average elector has more sound common sense than he is given credit for by people like the present Marquis of Salisbury (who has been foremost in the demand for the strengthening of the House of Lords). He is not swayed by oratory, and he is suspicious of fine promises. He is essentially conservative because in our social system he fears the consequence of extensive changes. In truth, politicians at the other extreme are equally mistaken in their political psychology. The political organisers of the Labour party have discovered by experience that the "inevitability of gradualism" is a law applying to elections as well as to administration. The trade unions are suspicious of "intellectuals" who want to do too much and too quickly; and even if the Labour party adopted truly revolutionary proposals, the only result would be that even more substantial sections of the working class would vote Conservative. What is more, no election can be won by the votes of the industrial workers alone. The lower middle class, which holds the balance, is the most conservative and most timid section of the population. It fears change because things might be worse. It does not follow that the present tendency to transfer capital from the wealthy to the State will not continue; but if the argument is that the wealthy classes ought to be protected, it leads to the conclusion that what is required is a dictatorship, not a Conservative majority in the House of Lords. If we want a democracy we must inevitably "trust the people".

§ 2. *The Need for a Second Chamber*

An argument that the House of Lords ought not to have a permanent Conservative majority is not necessarily an argument that there ought not to be a House of Lords. It would not be impossible to provide a Second Chamber giving a better representation of national interests and aspirations. The question whether such a Chamber is desirable depends on the functions which the House of Lords performs or could perform.

It must be remembered that the House performs some functions which are not usually given to a Second Chamber. It is, for instance, the final Court of Appeal for many legal causes arising in the United Kingdom. It was intended in 1873 to abolish this jurisdiction and legislation was passed for the purpose; but as a result of a change of Government the decision was reversed and the legislation repealed. Instead, authority was given for the appointment of paid "Lords of Appeal in Ordinary" who hold life peerages and sit in the House of Lords as ordinary members. The House of Lords for judicial business is in reality, though not in law, a different body from the House of Lords for legislative business, and it would be possible to abolish the latter without abolishing the former. Much the same argument applies to the jurisdiction which the House has as a court of first instance, for peerage cases and for the trial of peers accused of felony.

In the second place, the House debates general issues of policy. These debates are often very good. They are short, and few peers take part. Those who do are generally the peers with experience as minister, Governor-General of a Dominion or of India, ambassador, or otherwise. There are silly speeches in the House of Lords as in the House of Commons: but a peer rarely speaks for the sake of speaking. There is no necessity to "keep the debate going"; there are no constituents to demand frequent intervention; there are no great advantages to be obtained from publicity. Moreover, there is usually no division at the end; and if there is it does not matter, because the Government pays no attention whether to victory or to defeat. On the other hand, with the present House most of the debate is on one side if it is carried on for very long, because neither party in Opposition has more than a handful of speakers. These debates are useful but not essential. If the House were more representative they might be even more useful. In this respect, then, there would be some loss if the House were abolished.

In the third place, the House acts as a legislative chamber. Bills can be introduced there instead of in the House of Commons. The Bryce Committee stated in 1918 that Bills dealing with subjects of a partially non-controversial character may have an easier passage through the House of Commons if they have been fully discussed and put into a well-considered shape before being submitted to it. Government Bills ought, of course, to be in a well-considered shape before they are submitted to Parliament at all. It is nevertheless true that many amendments are made after publication because of representations made by "pressure groups" and other interested parties. The amendments are proposed by the Government, and in such cases the House of Lords merely ratifies them. Occasionally, also, useful amendments are suggested by peers—the "law lords", for instance, sometimes secure improvements in measures of law reform. Most amendments proposed by peers (like most amendments proposed by members of the House of Commons) are, however, either futile or destructive. When a Liberal or Labour Government is in power the result is to increase the time occupied in legislation in the House of Commons. Nevertheless, the statement of the Bryce Committee is substantially correct, though no great emphasis must be placed upon it. Bills are sometimes introduced by peers. They are comparatively rare, because the British Parliament has long ago learned that its task is primarily to criticise legislative proposals, not to initiate them. They cannot pass the Commons unless they are entirely non-controversial or are supported by the Government: but occasionally a Bill presented by a peer does get through.

Fourthly, the House of Lords debates Bills brought up from the House of Commons. This is the function in the exercise of which the House of Lords has most laid itself open to attack. Before 1911 the only remedy available to a Liberal Government was to threaten to create enough peers to give the Government a majority. Obviously the remedy could be used only in extreme cases. It was used in 1712 to pass the Treaty of Utrecht, in 1832 to pass the Reform Bill, and in 1911 to pass the Parliament Bill. It is such an extreme remedy that it can be used only where the King can be definitely assured that the measure has popular support; it thus demands a preliminary general election and its use obstructs all business for several months. Moreover, if the Government's bluff were called, the result would be effectively to destroy the House of Lords altogether. If the peers had not given way in 1911 the peerage would practically have been doubled; and the creation of enough peers by a Labour Government would now give the House of Lords a membership of 1500.

In 1911, however, the Parliament Act gave an additional remedy. The occasion for that Act was the rejection by the House of Lords of the Finance Bill of 1909 which gave effect to Mr Lloyd George's "confiscatory" land-tax Budget. The House had never before refused to pass a Finance Bill and it was alleged that to do so was to infringe the privilege of the House of Commons to be the sole judge of financial measures (though, apart from history, there is no compelling reason why a money Bill should be treated differently from any other Bill). Accordingly, the Parliament Act enables a money Bill to be presented for the royal assent and become law if it is not passed by the House of Lords within one month of its receipt. Conservative criticisms have propagated the notion that this provision creates a very wide breach in the power of the peers. It is said, for instance, that socialist provisions can be "tacked" to a money Bill. Actually, the term "money Bill" is very strictly defined, and it has been very rigidly interpreted by successive Speakers. The accusation really is that in a Labour Parliament Mr Speaker might be so biased as to allow tacking; but all history is against partial Speakers, and there is no more reason why Mr Speaker should so demean the high traditions of his office than there is why a judge should do so. Somebody, somewhere, must take the decision; and Mr Speaker has the advantage of a thorough knowledge of parliamentary procedure and the practice of legislation.

The provision as to money Bills is thus of comparatively minor importance. It really covers the Consolidated Fund Bills which grant money to the Crown (and which are never amended by the House of Commons), certain other minor Bills which are rarely controversial, and less than half of the Finance Bills which impose taxation (actually, twelve out of the twenty-nine Finance Bills between 1913 and 1937). It will be noted, however, that for this branch of legislation we have in practice single-chamber government.

In respect of other public Bills (except Bills to extend the duration of Parliament) the House of Lords can

interpose a delay of two years. In the meantime the
Bill must pass the House of Commons in three successive sessions. This does not mean that the time taken in
the House is tripled. In the period 1912 to 1914, when
this power was in process of use, the discussions on the
second and third occasions were rigidly limited. Nevertheless, it would add considerably to the labours of the
House of Commons under a Liberal or Labour Government. Moreover, two years is roughly half the lifetime
of a normal Parliament. The three sessions need not be
all in the same Parliament, but it is essential to a Government which makes promises at one election that it shall
be able to point to fulfilment at the next. Passing
legislation through the House of Commons is not
fulfilment. If the Labour party, for instance, promises
advantages from the nationalisation of the banks, the
mines, the railways and electricity supply (as it did in
1935), it must be able to show (say in 1939, if it had got
a majority and there had been no war) that these advantages have been obtained. If every one of these Bills
had to be passed under the Parliament Act, it is reasonably certain that there would be no results. Each would
take months of preparation, involving long conferences
in the Departments and in Cabinet committees, negotiations with outside bodies, and finally drafting. Each
would then take several months in the House of Commons, unless the "gag" was so seriously imposed that
the Opposition could reasonably complain of "dictatorship" at the next election. Then each would be delayed
two years by the House of Lords. In the interval it is
certain that the Opposition would not assist in speeding
up the procedure in the second and third sessions in
the House of Commons. Finally, there would be the
long administrative process of setting up new public
bodies, appointing staff, taking over functions, and the
like. No attempt at economies by rationalising pro-

duction and distribution and avoiding the waste of competition could be carried out before the Government found itself before the country once more—even making the large assumption that there were no political crises and no international complications during the lifetime of the Parliament.

It follows that this provision, too, is of very little value. It is unnecessary for a Conservative Government. It is almost completely obstructive for any other Government. Nor do the Opposition parties admit the moral right of the House of Lords to interpose so much delay. Actually, the provision has not been used except between 1912 and 1914, and neither of the two Acts then passed under it took effect as passed. The primary reason was that a war intervened; but the need for amending one of them was clear before it had finally passed; and it is evident that Bills changing social and economic conditions may often need amendment before two years have elapsed.

If we leave aside the special problem arising where the House of Lords rejects or amends a Bill promoted by a radical government, the amending power is still substantial. Fewer amendments are normally made in the House of Lords than in the House of Commons. Moreover, a much higher proportion is due to the Government's initiative. Indeed, many amendments are made in the House of Lords to meet criticisms advanced in the House of Commons. The peers' own amendments are few and unimportant, and no great loss would be suffered if they had no power to produce them. On the other hand, it is necessary to provide some means by which the Government amendments could be made. The "cleaning-up" process which goes on after the Bill has left the Commons is a valuable stage. The fact that so many amendments are made is not conclusive, because if there were no House of Lords most

of them would be made in the Commons. Moreover, if
there were a third House we would find another batch
of amendments, because however good a Bill may be it
can always be improved. It would be possible, by means
of a drafting committee or otherwise, to provide for
"cleaning-up" in the House of Commons. It must in
any case be done somewhere, and provisions for that
purpose would have to be made if the House of Lords
were abolished.

Finally, the House of Lords undertakes technical
functions which are important but seldom mentioned in
this connection. Half the local and private Bills are
examined in the first instance by committees of the
House of Lords. Such Bills undergo a "quasi-judicial"
process which may take much time when they are
opposed. A Bill opposed in one House is usually not
opposed in the other; and the result is that the peers
diminish by perhaps one-third the heavy and un-
interesting labours which would have to be undertaken
by members in the Commons if there were no House of
Lords. Provisional orders are in much the same position, and they are very common in Scotland. Other
orders are often considered by committees in the House
of Lords, though they pass in the Commons without
any formal scrutiny. In view of the increase in delegated
legislation, and the abuses which are possible (though
not common) in respect of it, this function is very
desirable.

In sum, therefore, the House of Lords exercises
functions which are generally recognised to be useful
though not absolutely necessary. Controversy reigns
only over the power to reject and delay. The power is
valuable only to Conservatives and for them only so
long as the House of Lords has a Conservative majority.
If the Government in power always had a majority, the
House of Lords would be as innocuous as it is now

under a Conservative Government. For those who are not Conservative, therefore, the choice can be made among three systems—a reformed House of Lords in which the Government always has a majority; a House of Lords (whether reformed or not) which has no power to reject or delay; and no Second Chamber at all. The Labour party asked in 1935 for a mandate to abolish the House of Lords, though it did not specifically say that it would not be replaced by another Second Chamber. The difficulties of securing such a change—whether by creation of peers or under the Parliament Act—are considerable. It would require a complex measure making provision for the exercise of functions now possessed by the House of Lords and worthy of continuance somewhere. A much simpler measure would be simply to extend the provision applying to money Bills—that is, one month's delay—to all public Bills. It could probably not be enacted except by a creation of peers or after two years' delay under the Parliament Act, but it would be a simple one-clause Bill. The question of the composition of the House of Lords could then be considered at leisure and no doubt it would be easier to reach agreement once the wings of the House had been clipped.

The problem of the House of Lords is, however, essentially controversial and the experience of the Constitutional Conference of 1910, which lasted for six months, and of the Bryce Committee of 1917–18, shows that no agreement could be reached even before the Labour party attained to the eminence of the second party in the State. It is even less capable of solution by agreement to-day.

CHAPTER V

THE MONARCHY

The difficulty of explaining the process of government lies in the fact that it depends so much on intangible relationships which are more easily felt than analysed. This is particularly true of the Crown. On the one hand it is easy to exaggerate the influence of the monarchy by adopting a legalistic attitude and emphasising the part played by the Crown in the theory of constitutional law. On the other hand it is easy to minimise the royal function by stressing the great trilogy of Cabinet, Parliament and People. The truth lies somewhere in between, but it is not a truth easily demonstrated, nor is it constant in its content. So much depends on private interviews which political scientists do not attend, and so much on the personalities of those who do attend.

The King has one, and only one, function of primary importance. It is to appoint a Prime Minister. Somewhere in every constitution founded on responsible government there must be someone who takes the first step to form a new Government when a gap is threatened. Inevitably that function is exercised here by the King. Frequently it is almost automatic. When the Conservative party secured a majority at the general election of 1924, there could be no doubt that Mr Baldwin had to be Prime Minister. If a party secures a majority and that party has a leader, that leader must become Prime Minister. If and when the Labour party secures a majority, there can never be any doubt, because the party always insists on the right of the Labour members of Parliament to choose their own leader. The Conservative party does not follow this practice. Mr Baldwin became leader in 1923 and Mr Chamberlain in 1937 because they were Prime Ministers. The formality of election—now by a meeting of Conservative members, peers and candidates—was in each case followed, but it was a mere formality, an expression of confidence in the leader chosen by the King. What would happen if the party became leaderless when in Opposition cannot precisely be determined because the question has not arisen since 1911. In that year Mr Bonar Law was elected leader, not of the party but of the Conservative members of Parliament, the leadership of the party being left open until 1922, when he became Prime Minister. This is in substance the Labour practice, except that the leader of the Parliamentary Labour party is elected annually. On the other hand, it is not a satisfactory method for the Conservative party, because the party leader is in control of the Conservative Central Office—a body which, it has already been explained, has no equivalent in the Labour party.

The King thus has a choice when the Conservative party has a majority but no leader, or when no party has a majority. In the former case, his duty is to appoint a Prime Minister who will command the willing support of the party majority. Where a Prime Minister retires, it may be assumed that he will advise as to his successor. It is true that Queen Victoria did not ask Gladstone's advice in 1894. She had already decided to send for Lord Rosebery. It would have been better if she had asked because she would at least have heard of the difficulties involved in appointing this "dark horse in a loose box".

Nor is it certain that Edward VII asked Lord Salisbury's advice in 1902, though Balfour's accession was so obvious that advice was hardly necessary. Again in 1908 it appears that Edward VII did not consult Campbell-Bannerman; but Asquith had been presiding over the Cabinet during the Prime Minister's illness. No information is available as to the appointment of Mr Chamberlain in 1937, but it is a reasonable presumption that Mr Baldwin had been consulted.

These examples show how frequently a successor is clearly indicated by the political situation. In Lord Rosebery's case, the succession was almost inevitable. In some cases, however, there is no inevitability. If, for instance, Mr Chamberlain had resigned in March 1939 owing to the failure of the Munich policy, who would have succeeded him—Sir Samuel Hoare, Sir John Simon, Sir Kingsley Wood or Lord Halifax? Such a problem arose on the resignation of Bonar Law in 1923. Lord Curzon was the only minister with long experience, because most of the Coalition Unionists had gone out with Mr Lloyd George in 1922. Mr Baldwin was the obvious candidate from the House of Commons, but his Cabinet experience was limited to the eight months of the Bonar Law Government, and until the Conservative revolt of October 1922 he had been at most a quite obscure junior minister. Apart from the defects of Lord Curzon's character immortalised in the lines—

> George Nathaniel, Viscount Curzon,
> Is really a very superior person,

he was a peer. Lord Rosebery and Lord Salisbury had led governments from the House of Lords; but, in the first place, these precedents were not happy, especially Lord Rosebery's; and, in the second place, the position was now different because the Labour party was the official Opposition and was practically unrepresented in the House of Lords. George V thus had a very difficult problem to solve. After consulting several Conservative statesmen, he decided, rightly as is generally thought, to summon Mr Baldwin.

The function is equally important where no party has a majority or the position is otherwise complicated. Thus, on the resignation of Mr Baldwin's Government on its defeat in the House of Commons, after a general election, in 1924, George V was called upon to decide whether to summon Mr Asquith, as leader of the Liberal party, or Mr Ramsay MacDonald, as leader of the Labour party, or some other person who might, perhaps, try to form a coalition. He decided to send for Mr MacDonald, who in fact had behind him only about one-third of the members of the House. The events of 1931 were even more complicated. The Labour Government, which had no majority, had resigned, and the country was passing through what was called a financial crisis. A general election was out of the question and the Labour party was the largest party in the House. The King commissioned Mr MacDonald to form a coalition, though it is not clear whether the suggestion came from the King, Mr MacDonald, or Mr Baldwin. The King was much criticised for this action; but there is no evidence that he acted unconstitutionally. The action of Mr MacDonald, on the other hand, is not easy to defend. Finally, it is enough to notice the problem created in May 1940, because the process by which Mr Churchill became Prime Minister has not been disclosed. Probably Mr Churchill's name arose in discussions between Mr Chamberlain and the Opposition leaders.

Such examples do not occur very frequently, but they show the importance of the function. The King is in a favourable position because he is in close contact with the Government, though he rarely has opportunity for studying Opposition leaders, particularly where, as with the Labour party in 1939, they have been out of office for a long period. At the same time he is, or ought to be, impartial. Even monarchs have their prejudices, as Queen Victoria showed; but at least they are less partisan than active politicians.

In many other cases the King exercises functions, but for the most part they are formal. He is present at Privy Council meetings when the more important kinds of delegated legislation are passed. He appoints ministers, ambassadors, judges, military, naval and air force officers, senior civil servants, and so on. He summons and dissolves Parliament. He creates peers, and confers honours. He assents to legislation. In nearly every case he acts on the "advice" of ministers; that is, the effective decision is that of the Cabinet, the Prime Minister or the Departmental minister concerned. Where a formal act is required he is obviously in a position to ask for explanations and to give advice. The Privy Council is a purely formal body and no discussion takes place. If, however, a Draft Order in Council is brought up, the minister concerned usually attends. Either before or after the meeting, therefore, the King can ask for an explanation. There have been occasions when items have been postponed because the King wished for explanations.

Even where no formal act is required, however, the King can ask for explanations and give advice. He receives a copy of the Cabinet "minutes" and also of the "daily print" of despatches circulated by the Foreign Office. He follows debates in Parliament by means of the *Official Report*. These supplement the information which he receives from newspapers, from personal inspections, and from interviews. Moreover, he has a staff to keep him informed of the developments of political life. For these reasons, if he chooses to devote himself to the study of affairs, he can soon acquire a considerable knowledge of British politics. Though personally remote from Parliament and platform, he is constantly close to the scene of great events.

His capacity to influence them depends upon his personal qualities. It would be unreasonable to expect that he will be more than an ordinary man. The Hanoverians were not chosen for their intellectual qualities, and in any case no family produces a genius in every generation in the direct line of descent. Neither George V nor George VI would lay claim to more than industry and common sense. These, however, are qualities which, if used at the centre of affairs, can be extremely valuable. Few of our ministers are more than plain men. The nation could throw up thousands of men as competent as Mr Baldwin or Mr Chamberlain. In fact, the British people has a suspicion of intellect and imagination, except in war time. The King, like a minister, has a part to play in public. Like the President of the French Republic he has to be a *bon bourgeois*. Unlike a minister, however, he is not compelled to maintain a glib assurance in matters of politics. He has no cause to be a partisan, and there is no tendency for him to be satisfied with the slick slogans that sometimes muster as arguments. The besetting sin of politicians is that they tend to believe what they say. A little grain of salt in public life is often salutary. A king like George V and a statesman like Mr Baldwin could hobnob as equals. A king like George V could puncture Mr Lloyd George's rhetoric (unless he were carried away by it, which also is possible) as a pin punctures a balloon. Mr Gladstone, complained Queen Victoria, "addresses me as if I were a public meeting". She was the most chilling of his audiences, though she succumbed, as no public meeting ever did, to Disraeli's blandishments. A king who can keep his head (metaphorically) can do immense good, simply by injecting a little common sense.

On occasions, something more is required. The right

of dissolution, for instance, is not solely within the competence of the Prime Minister. A king who thought that the power was being put to serious abuse could refuse to allow a dissolution. The occasion has not recently arisen in this country, though in 1910 there was some hesitation. In the Dominions, however, the problem has at times been acute. If a Prime Minister advised a dissolution merely because he was no longer in agreement with the majority of his colleagues—like General Hertzog in 1939—the King would be fully entitled to refuse. If Mr Chamberlain had (as he would not in fact have thought of doing) advised a dissolution in May 1940, when the Germans were crossing the Albert canal, the King would have been justified in refusing.

In other words, there are occasions when the "formal" functions cease to be merely formal. Normally, the king would not refuse to grant a peerage to any person recommended by the Prime Minister, though he would be entitled to make representations if the character of the person seemed to make a peerage unfitting. He would not, however, allow 750 peers to be created in order to give a majority in the House of Lords unless he felt that public opinion really demanded it. He might thus require, as in 1910, that a general election be held on this specific issue.

The fundamental principle which governs his action in such a case is that his prerogative is not to be used for purely partisan ends. He himself must neither be nor seem to be a partisan. Unionist politicians in 1913 demanded that George V dissolve Parliament without "advice" from the Liberal Government. The demand was foolish because, though the king's co-operation is necessary for a dissolution, ministerial co-operation is equally necessary. It therefore could be regarded only as a demand for the king to dismiss his ministers on the specious argument that they had no "mandate" for

Home Rule. Had George V acted in this way, he would have shown himself to be a partisan, to be, in other words, a Unionist.

It must be emphasised, however, that these problems are exceptional. Far more important than the king's governmental functions are what Bagehot calls his "dignified" functions. The process of government is not a question merely of securing loyalty and efficiency in the public services. Vast tracts of government are with us left to unpaid amateurs. Peers, aldermen, councillors, magistrates, members of Royal Commissions and advisory committees, the thousands of persons engaged in voluntary social services and philanthropic societies give their time and experience to the public weal. Nor is this all. Government is not just a matter of giving orders and enforcing obedience. It requires the willing collaboration of all sections of the people. Moreover, democracy is government by the people as well as for the people. Individuals must feel a personal responsibility for the collective action.

To say all this is merely to say that patriotism within limits—the kind of patriotism which is co-operative and not aggressive—is an admirable principle. A people at war cannot fail to be impressed with its importance; but it is equally important in time of peace. It is of course not necessary to have a monarchy to have patriotism. The Fifth Column has been found in monarchies, and the two greatest republics in the world are not deficient in patriotism. Nevertheless, a monarchy provides a useful focus for patriotism, particularly where it has a long and glorious history. If England had remained a republic after 1648, or had become a republic in 1688, it would by now have acquired that aurora of sentiment which attaches to *la patrie* or the Constitution of the United States. Until 1760 the Stuarts carried more "romance" than the Georges.

Nevertheless, the more concrete the symbol the more effective it is. The State functions more easily if it can be personified. An elected President who has stepped out of politics, like the French President, is no substitute for a king who has stepped in by right of inheritance (even if, like George VI, he stepped in because his predecessor stepped out). Still less is an active politician, like the President of the United States, a substitute. We can damn the Government and cheer the king.

This personification of the State in the king requires, to be fully effective, that the king be active in good works. Gladstone rightly complained of Queen Victoria's retirement for many years after the death of the Prince Consort. The effect of Disraeli's persuasion was visible at the Jubilee of 1887 and the Diamond Jubilee of 1897. The "little old lady" caught the popular imagination just when the extension of the franchise required the popular imagination to be stimulated. Perhaps, indeed, it was a little too inflamed. It may be that Milner and Joseph Chamberlain could not have had their war in South Africa if the line between patriotism and jingoism had not been crossed.

This is, however, a matter of opinion on which no impartial observer could be dogmatic. Certain it is that democratic government is not merely a matter of cold reason and prosaic policies. There must be some display of colour, and there is nothing more vivid than royal purple and imperial scarlet. During the present century, therefore, we have placed almost an intolerable burden on the royal family. They must not only head subscription lists and appear on State occasions; they must, also, inspect this and that, open this and that, lay this stone and that, and undertake a thousand other dull tasks in a blaze of publicity. We can hardly blame Edward VIII if he preferred to make toffee in the kitchen. George V had made himself a slave to the public demand.

The medieval "romance" which surrounds the king is not, however, without its disadvantages. Patriotism can easily slop over into jingoism, though there has been very little evidence of it in the present century. Moreover, the methods adopted by the royal entourage, and acquiesced in (perhaps unwillingly) by the royal family, tend to perpetuate that social stratification which is so inconsistent with democracy. The main cause is the maldistribution of wealth, and it is assisted by the public-school system and the steepness of the educational ladder. Nevertheless, the flaunting of wealth in levees, "courts", garden parties and the Royal Enclosure plays a part. The contrast with the Dominions and the United States is most obvious. Moreover, it is completely unnecessary. It is a mere relic of past ages, maintained by the royal family on the advice of persons who, well-intentioned though they are, have not sufficiently realised that a monarchy, too, must change with the times. It is this atmosphere of class distinction which makes some suspicious of the monarchy as an institution. It appears to give substance to that phantom of the "class war" which plays such a large part in current political controversy. Those who want to abolish all "circuses" are not entirely accurate in their appreciation of mass psychology. No objection need be raised to great ceremonies like the Coronation, the State opening of Parliament, Jubilee celebrations, and the Changing of the Guard. The public plays a part in these, if only as spectators lining the route. For the rest, there would be gain if some of the "flummery" were dispensed with.

It would be improper to end this survey of "dignified" functions without reference to the part played by the Crown as the link in the British Commonwealth of Nations. It has relevance rather to that peculiarly British institution than to the British Constitution itself. The monarchy is, however, part of the contribution made

The King opens Parliament

by the senior partner. The king has formal functions in
relation to the Dominions and India. In so far as the
government of India is the concern of the British
Government, he can exercise the same influence as on
any other aspect of British policy. Moreover, as formal
head of the State for all the Dominions except Eire he
is able to take a Commonwealth rather than a purely
British (i.e. English and Scottish) view of Commonwealth
relations and to influence the Government at Westminster accordingly. Nevertheless, his main function is
to act as a "symbol of the free association of the members
of the British Commonwealth of Nations"—to use the
language of the preamble to the Statute of Westminster.
Subordination to the Government at Westminster would
be inconsistent with Dominion status. Common "allegiance" to the Crown is not. Thus a unity based on free
association and sentiment can be preserved by a legal
fiction in spite of independence and frequently divergent
interests.

CHAPTER VI

ADMINISTRATION

§ 1. *Administrative Bodies*

Parliament and political parties operate for the most part in the light of day. They are, so to speak, constitutional instruments of publicity. The ordinary individual therefore has a substantially accurate notion of the part they play. The delicate balance of relationships and the degree of emphasis to be given to functions are matters for the practical politician and the expert; but the elector is fully entitled to make up his mind on their utility and efficiency. Knowledge of the working of the Cabinet system is less widespread because so much of it is secret. Yet the Cabinet occupies the centre of the stage. It is "the Government" which is blamed if things go awry and—more rarely—praised if things go well. Its members are in Parliament and are leaders of the parties. Its actions arouse public interest and its functions are well known. It is necessary to emphasise, however, that the British Constitution would not work at all if there were not thousands of less publicised persons engaged in the detailed working of the institutions of government.

The complexity of the British system of administration arises partly from history, but above all from the wide range of functions which it has to fulfil. It must be remembered in the first place that in Northern Ireland much of the administration is conducted under the control of the Parliament of Northern Ireland and not under that of the United Kingdom. Consequently, there is an administrative system quite distinct from that of Great Britain. In the second place, the administrative systems of England and Scotland have never been completely assimilated, so that generally speaking the Ministry of Health, the Ministry of Agriculture and Fisheries, and the Board of Education exercise functions in relation to England only. There are separate Departments in Scotland under the general control of the Secretary of State for Scotland, who also has some functions which in England are exercised by the Home Secretary. There are, further, two distinct sets of local government institutions. Finally, the judicial systems are distinct, with the result that the administrative apparatus which they require is divided, the Lord Chancellor exercises functions in England only, and there are two sets of Law Officers.

It must also be emphasised that it is not easy to determine where "administration" ends and "private enterprise" begins. There is, for instance, the whole group of public utilities, such as railways, tramways, docks, canals, water undertakings, gas undertakings, electricity undertakings, and the rest. They are all regulated under special powers conferred by Parliament, though some are governed by local authorities, some by companies, and some by commissions. In this field "company" usually indicates private enterprise; but it is not uncommon for Parliament to authorise the formation of a company (such as "Unco") simply as an instrument of government. Purely governmental functions are also exercised by other bodies, sometimes mere voluntary associations: examples are the Law Society, the General Medical Council, the Dental Board, the Architects' Registration Council, and the Nurses' Registration Council. It is very difficult to know where to place such bodies as the British Broadcasting Corporation, the London Passenger Transport Board, the Central

Electricity Board, the Metropolitan Water Board, the Port of London Authority, Trinity House, catchment boards, drainage boards, marketing boards, the Spindles Board, the Wheat Commission, and so on. The explanation is, as usual, that the British Constitution is essentially empirical. An existing body is given a new function, or an old function is transferred to a new body, or a new body is created to exercise a new function, simply as it appears most convenient at the time. The growth in the functions of the State has caused hundreds of new bodies to be created, and has conferred new duties on hundreds of existing bodies. No general principles run through administrative law. Their methods of organisation, their powers, and the extent to which they exercise them, are known only to those who are specially concerned with each group.

Fortunately, now that they have been mentioned they can be ignored. They certainly create difficult problems, particularly in their relation to other branches of government. From a social or economic angle they cannot be ignored, because many of them have powers of compulsion or of monopoly which closely affect the interests of ordinary people. We shall soon reach the stage where it can seriously be asked whether we have democracy when we are governed by a vast array of boards, commissions, corporations, companies, authorities, councils, and the rest, whose relation to Parliament or to a local electorate is remote. Problems of this order must, however, be discussed either at length or not at all. They are different in respect of each social function.

For our present purpose, also, we can ignore the local authorities. It must certainly be remembered that they exercise some of the most important and the most intimate functions of the State. It has been well said that modern civilisation rests on drains and sewers; and local authorities are not concerned with public health alone, but also with education, police, housing, planning, and the rest. There are problems here, too, but they are much less urgent and no less technical than those relating to other minor bodies. The fact that local authorities are directly responsible to the people solves the major difficulty.

The essential problems of a general order are those that relate to the central Departments of State, which function under the control of ministers responsible to Parliament. Here, too, the consequences of increasing State functions are obvious. At the beginning of the eighteenth century the Departments of State were the Lord Chancellor's Department, the Treasury, the Privy Council Office, the Privy Seal Office, the Admiralty, the Offices of the two Secretaries of State, the War Office, and the Post Office. All these (except the Privy Seal Office, which exercised entirely redundant functions) remain. The Offices of the two Secretaries of State have expanded into the Foreign Office, the Home Office, the Dominions Office, the Colonial Office, the India Office, the Burma Office and the Scottish Office. The War Office and the Air Ministry also have Secretaries of State. In addition there are the Board of Trade, the Board of Education, the Ministry of Agriculture and Fisheries, the Ministry of Labour, the Ministry of Health, the Ministry of Transport, the Ministry of Pensions, and the Office of Works; and in war time there are even more—the Ministry of Supply, the Ministry of Food, the Ministry of Information, the Ministry of Shipping, the Ministry of Economic Warfare and the Ministry of Aircraft Production.

It is not easy to generalise about these numerous bodies, because it is fallacious to assume that their functions are in all respects equivalent. Their methods of organisation are different because they have to undertake tasks of a very dissimilar character. It is unnecessary to discuss the special war-time Departments. In part they exercise functions which are peculiar to war. In totalitarian war the State exercises wider powers of control than it has as yet assumed in time of peace. These include the powers of the Ministry of Supply over raw materials, those of the Ministry of Food over the importation and distribution of foodstuffs, and those of the Ministry of Shipping. Some functions are purely belligerent, such as those of the Ministries of Economic Warfare and of Information. Others, such as the purchasing functions of the Ministry of Supply and the Ministry of Aircraft Production, are merely peace-time functions enormously expanded. The peace-time Departments similarly have special war-time functions, as the expansion of the Ministry of Labour into the Ministry of Labour and National Service, and of the addition to the Home Office of the Ministry of Home Security, indicate.

Leaving these special functions aside, the Departments may be classified as follows:

(1) *Defence*. The Admiralty, the War Office and the Air Ministry provide for the civilian control of the armed forces. Their functions include the raising of the forces by voluntary enlistment, the provision of equipment, armaments, munitions and other stores (whether by purchase or by direct manufacture in ordnance factories and Government shipyards), the allocation of forces, and the provision of accommodation. They necessarily require technical knowledge, so that the Departments employ in their administration not only civil servants but also officers of the three services. In fact, the supreme body in each, subject to the ultimate control of the minister, is a committee in which senior officers predominate—the Board of Admiralty, the Army Council and the Air Council.

(2) *External Relations*. The Foreign Office is one of the simplest organisations because its functions are to a substantial degree of a "political" order. Though it has the

Diplomatic and the Consular Services under its control, it has not to take such a vast number of technical decisions as most Departments. Its main task is to collect information on which political decisions can be taken by the Foreign Secretary or the Cabinet. The Dominions Office similarly is concerned more with policy than with technical decisions. In fact, its lower branches are shared with the Colonial Office. That Office is primarily concerned with the recruitment of the various colonial services and with control over the decisions of colonial governors and other administrators. The India and Burma Offices have functions of the same kind, though each is concerned with a single Government only. The two Offices are amalgamated both at the top and at the bottom. The differentiation arises only among the very senior civil servants. It may be noted that functions of a similar order are exercised by the Home Office in relation to the Channel Islands and the Isle of Man.

(3) *Administrative Control.* Since many of the functions of the State are exercised by the numerous bodies outside the central administrative system, powers of control are exercised by central Departments. Thus, the Board of Education has control powers over local education authorities. The Ministry of Transport has powers of control in respect of the highway functions of local authorities, over the transport undertakings of local authorities and other bodies (including railway companies), and, through the Electricity Commissioners, over the Central Electricity Board and electricity undertakings. The Board of Trade has similar functions over gas undertakings and dock and harbour undertakings. The Ministry of Agriculture and Fisheries has control powers over the agricultural powers of local authorities, over catchment boards and drainage boards, and over the special boards and commissions created in recent years for dealing with various agricultural and fishery problems. The Home Office controls the police, fire brigade and local election machinery. The other control functions over local government are vested in the Ministry of Health. In many cases, it will be realised, there is a differentiation in Scotland, where the Scottish Office or a Department under

its control takes the place of the appropriate English Department.

(4) *Direct Services*. If we omit the defence services, the oldest service which is provided directly for the benefit of citizens is the Post Office. In recent times, however, there have been notable extensions of these services. The Ministry of Labour provides the system of employment exchanges and administers directly the Unemployment Insurance system, and it also has power of control over the Assistance Board which provides unemployment assistance, and supplementary pensions for widows and aged people. The Ministry of Health similarly administers the National Health Insurance system and the Widows', Orphans' and Old Age Contributory Pensions system. The Ministry of Pensions provides war pensions. A service which can hardly be described without explanation as for the benefit of citizens is the prisons system, which is operated by the Prison Commission under the control of the Home Office. The Home Office also has direct control over the Metropolitan Police.

(5) *Law Enforcement*. Law enforcement is primarily the concern of the police, who are employed outside the Metropolitan Police Area by the local authorities and standing joint committees. It sometimes requires, however, much more positive administration, such as frequent inspection. Much of this also is done by local authorities, such as the branches relating to weights and measures and food and drugs. The Home Office is the controlling body. But sometimes a central Department is directly concerned. Factory inspection and the control of explosives and aliens are under the Home Office, though the Ministry of Labour is concerned with the employment of aliens and also (in war time) with factory inspection. The inspection of mines, etc. is under the control of the Mines Department of the Board of Trade, while the Board of Trade is directly concerned with merchant shipping, bankruptcy, companies and the like. The Ministry of Agriculture and Fisheries is concerned with plant and animal diseases.

(6) *Assistance to Private Enterprise*. This function cannot easily be differentiated from the others, because it tends to

develop into enforcement or control. Thus, the Ministry of Agriculture and Fisheries was primarily concerned, until recently, with assistance to farmers and fishermen. Demands arose, however, for financial and not merely technical assistance, and financial assistance involved control. Consequently, the character of the Ministry has changed. Similarly, the Mines Department was concerned with assistance and enforcement, but now has powers of control through the Coal Commission and (in peace time) the Petroleum Board. The Board of Trade and the Ministry of Agriculture and Fisheries still assist by the provision of information and in other ways.

(7) *Ancillary Services*. The greatest of the ancillary services is the provision of money and the control of all Government expenditure. This is the special function of the Treasury, which raises taxation through the Commissioners of Inland Revenue and of Customs and Excise. Money is also obtained from the Crown Lands Commission and the Post Office. Financial control also means control over Departmental estimates and over contracts. It has led, too, to general control by the Treasury over the Civil Service. Finally, the Office of Works provide the buildings and furniture required by the Government Departments and their numerous outposts.

It must not be thought that the above gives a complete survey of governmental functions. It does, however, illustrate their variety. It is enough to show that many classes of civil servants are required. The Post Office, for instance, employs postmen and men engaged in the carriage of mail, telephone and telegraph operators, engineers, sorters, counter assistants, an immense clerical staff engaged in checking, accounting, docketing, and the rest. The Admiralty dockyards, the ordnance factories and the Office of Works employ skilled, semi-skilled and unskilled workers. Professional men of all kinds—lawyers, accountants, architects, scientists, engineers—are to be found in some or all of the Departments.

Every Department requires shorthand typists, typists, cleaners, porters and messengers. Some of the clerical work demands a high degree of skill and knowledge, and is performed by what is known as the "executive class", while some is almost mechanical. There are special classes such as the inspectors, the customs and exise officers, the employment officers in the Employment Exchanges, and the inspectors of taxes. The ultimate decisions are taken by civil servants, under ministerial control, who require the highest intelligence that the nation can produce.

§ 2. *The Process of Administration*

Enough has been said to indicate that it is quite impossible to describe the process of administration. The citizen meets it at many points, the local post office, the telephone exchange, the employment exchange, the office of the inspector of taxes even, in London, at the street corner. The most important part, however, is that with which he is not directly in contact but which really influences his environment even more because it assists ministers in reaching the decisions which determine the policy of the country. This "administrative class", as it is called, is very small. In peace time it contains only about 1300 people, while Government employees of all classes number nearly 500,000 of whom about 150,000 are commonly designated as "civil servants" by ordinary citizens. These 1300 men and women, however, occupy the key positions in the administrative system. Some of them are so important that their names get into the newspapers in spite of the service practice of anonymity —Lord Hankey who, as Sir Maurice Hankey, was Secretary to the Cabinet, Clerk of the Privy Council, and Secretary to the Committee of Imperial Defence; Sir Horace Wilson, who is now Permanent Secretary to the

Treasury and Head of the Civil Service; Sir Warren
Fisher, his predecessor; Sir Robert Vansittart, Diplo-
matic Adviser to the Government; Sir Alexander
Cadogan, Permanent Under-Secretary of State for
Foreign Affairs; Sir F. W. Leggett of the Ministry of
Labour; Sir Findlater Stewart, Permanent Under-
Secretary of State for India, who recently spent some
months as Director-General of the Ministry of Information; Sir Frederick Leith-Ross, who is now Director-
General of the Ministry of Economic Warfare; and others
whose names the reader will recall. These are among the
most eminent of the administrative class; but that class
includes also the young men and women who came
straight from the Universities at the examination of 1939.

Many of these civil servants of the administrative
class are engaged upon what may be called internal
administrative tasks. They may be concerned, for instance, with financial relations with the Treasury, or with
appointments to and promotion in the civil service. Our
primary interest is in policy-making. It will therefore be
convenient to assume that the administrative class
exercises that function alone. If we take the hierarchical
system of a Department like the Ministry of Health, we
find that it is somewhat as follows:

The Minister.
    Private Secretary.
    Assistant Private Secretary.
        The Parliamentary Secretary.
            Private Secretary.
The Secretary.
    Private Secretary.
The Deputy Secretary.
    Private Secretary.
  8 Principal Assistant Secretaries.
13 Assistant Secretaries.
41 Principals.
21 Assistant Principals.

The Minister and the Parliamentary Secretary are members of Parliament. In some Departments the Parliamentary Secretary exercises some of the functions which would normally be exercised by the Minister, either because there is a traditional allocation (as with the Financial Secretaries to the War Office and the Admiralty) or because the Minister specially delegates certain of his functions (as Mr Lloyd George delegated to Mr Addison when he was Minister of Munitions). Generally speaking, however, the Parliamentary Secretary's functions are parliamentary; and inside the Department he is concerned partly to advise himself about the many problems which may arise in Parliament and partly to assist generally by commenting on documents and attending committee meetings.

The Secretary is the permanent head of the Department, and his position has been likened to that of a general manager. He exercises general control, he has the last word on proposals that go to the Minister, and the first word on proposals that come from the Minister. The Deputy Secretary gives general assistance to the Secretary and perhaps pays special attention to certain aspects of the Department's work. For instance, the Deputy Secretary to the Ministry of Health might be specially concerned with the preparation and passing of legislation.

The Principal Assistant Secretaries are concerned with the separate branches of the work of the Ministry. In the Ministry of Health, for instance, one deals with finance, another with the poor law, another with housing and town planning, and so on. Where the work is large, a Principal Assistant Secretary might be assisted by an Assistant Secretary. A less heavy section of the work might not require a Principal Assistant Secretary at all, but would be in charge of an Assistant Secretary. The Principals give these senior officials, as well as the senior technical officials, general assistance by writing memoranda, commenting on other people's memoranda, acting as secretaries to Departmental Committees, summarising the contents of files, analysing statistics, and so on. The Assistant Principals do the same kind of work, but they are younger and less experienced, and their main task is to learn the process which will fit some of them to become Permanent Secretaries. The Minister will probably have a Principal as private secretary, while the other private secretaries will probably be Assistant Principals.

The function with which we are here concerned is the taking and execution of decisions. Regarded from the angle of the civil service, this involves tasks of three kinds. First, there is the collection and analysis of information. The accumulated wisdom of the Government is to be found not merely in the minds of ministers and civil servants, nor even in the files of memoranda, but in the libraries of books, despatches, reports, and so on. Information on anything within the range of the Department may be required quickly. The Foreign Office provides the best example, because everybody knows that a constant succession of despatches comes in from British representatives abroad. The Foreign Secretary, the Permanent Under-Secretary, the Deputy Under-Secretary, perhaps even an Assistant Under-Secretary will have an interview with an ambassador or a minister or a counsellor of embassy or legation, and a note is promptly taken for purposes of record. Such foreign representatives may also bring or send documents. Newspapers and press-cuttings provide information which may be more or less accurate than that provided from official sources, but which must be read and checked. Eminent people (even professors) sometimes write books whose contents must be known. Not much of this information may be immediately relevant. Ruritania may be off the map, so far as the Foreign Office is concerned, for a decade. Suddenly, however, news comes that a delicate situation has arisen because the Crown Prince has been assassinated, or a general election has brought in an unfriendly Government, or some British subject has been imprisoned. At once everybody from the Prime Minister to an Assistant Secretary clamours for a full but concise account of the whole background. There has to be somebody in the Department who knows something about it and, above all, who knows exactly where in the files of the Department is to be found the material for a complete story. The informatory function is, it is believed, well exercised in the Foreign Office. In some other Departments conditions are not so good—perhaps because the Treasury does not like paying for Principals who read books and documents. It is believed, for instance, that the Ministry of Health has no collection of local authorities' minutes and agenda, which would indicate what the local authorities are actually doing.

The provision of information is an ancillary function without which action is likely to be bad because it is, so to speak, performed in the dark. The essential function of the administrative class is in the taking of decisions. In the days when the present Cabinet system was established, it was possible for a minister to take every important decision himself. We find Peel and Gladstone, for instance, corresponding not merely about the principle of tariff reduction, but about minutiae of detail. Sir James Graham at the Admiralty did not personally order the crew of a man-of-war to reef the topsail, but he knew everything that went on in the Admiralty. Lord John Russell and Gladstone drafted clauses in Bills. Every appointment was made in fact and not merely in form by a minister. He required only a principal adviser, a few technical officers and some clerical assistance.

This history is important, because it was under Peel, Russell and Gladstone that the theory of Cabinet Government was established. Yet in 1842 the national expenditure was in the region of fifty million pounds. The civil service, including all classes, could not have contained more than 40,000 people. In 1936 the national expenditure was about eight hundred million pounds and the civil service numbered practically 500,000. A ten-fold increase in the work does not mean that the minister takes ten times as many decisions, particularly when it is remembered that his parliamentary and political functions have also increased and that most of these cannot be delegated. It means that the modern minister takes few of the decisions, though the number varies from the Foreign Office, where so many are "political", to the Post Office, where the Postmaster-General takes very few.

Many decisions are of course purely matters of routine. When an unemployed insured person "registers", he is aware that the Minister of Labour personally knows nothing whatever about him, and that some minor official decides whether he is entitled to benefit. Even where there is a discretion the decision may be taken far down the hierarchy. A local officer of the Assistance Board has power to determine whether an unemployed person shall have slightly more than the official scale of unemployment assistance. Matters of wider importance, however, go up as far as an Assistant Secretary. A housing scheme, for instance, would ultimately receive the approval of such an official. Similarly, any question of principle would go as far. No person of a lower station than an Assistant Secretary would sign a document on behalf of a minister. Subject to any instructions that might be issued, a problem would be sent higher up only if it was of special difficulty, or was unusual, or might involve political controversy. If several branches of the Department were concerned, several persons would have remarks to make, and in the absence of agreement it might have to be brought before a Departmental Committee (which is not to be confused with a committee of outside persons appointed by the minister to make a report). If two or more Departments were concerned, it might be necessary to have an inter-Departmental Committee.

The great majority of questions are, however, "departmental questions". They involve the exercise of a wide and informed discretion. Formally, many of them will go to the minister. If he is wise, he will deal only with those which are indicated to be important. It is the duty of the Permanent Secretary to see that everything of importance is submitted to the minister. It is the minister who is responsible, and he if anybody will be criticised in the House of Commons. On the other hand, it is equally the duty of the Permanent Secretary to see that the minister is not bothered by questions of a minor order. The questions submitted to the minister are, however, more numerous than those which might strictly be called "political". Such questions, and such questions only, must ultimately be put before the Cabinet. This is particularly true of proposals involving substantial expenditure or the passing of new legislation, or which concern more than one Department, or which may be discussed in the House of Commons. The minister must be prepared to make positive proposals on these matters, and must therefore make up his own mind: but in addition he will consider questions of a departmental nature, perhaps involving administrative reorganisation, or a change of policy, or the appointment of a committee of investigation.

Thus, there is a hierarchy of decisions which may be classified as follows:

Routine and minor discretion.	Executive class.
Discretion within a policy.	Assistant Secretary.
Departmental policy.	Permanent Secretary and Minister.
Government policy.	Cabinet.

This is a very rough classification indeed, because the division cannot be expressed in words. The important fact is, however, that a very large number of decisions is taken by senior civil servants. Moreover, even if a decision is taken by the minister or by the Cabinet, the case must be prepared. The information available must be collected by a Principal or an Assistant Principal, who will, at least if he is asked to do so, add his suggestions as to the line to take. His memorandum will be read by an Assistant Secretary, who may send it forward with his comments, or throw it in the waste-paper basket and write another, or hand it over to another and more senior Principal with the request to put the information in a sensible form. Other Assistant Secretaries may have their remarks to make. The file may go to another Department for comment. Principal Assistant Secretaries, Deputy Secretaries and Permanent Secretaries may add words of agreement and disagreement. The files which preceded the introduction of the great local government reform in 1928, for instance, must have been extremely bulky. Knotty problems will be discussed by committees. Precisely where in this process the minister comes in depends partly on him and partly on the problem. At the end, however, there lies before him a definite statement of the practicable alternatives, with the arguments for and against each of them. He can see the files if he wishes, but generally there is no need, because the combined wisdom of the Department has brought the question down to an issue where common sense and political *savoir faire* are the qualities required. If he says that he must consult the Cabinet, he makes up his own mind and gets an Assistant Secretary (who perhaps gets a Principal) to state the case in a Cabinet memorandum.

Somewhere and eventually the decision is taken. Then comes the third function, that of execution. The higher the decision goes, the more general it is likely to be, and the greater the need for interpretation. A decision to raise the school-leaving age, for instance, would be taken by the Cabinet. That decision would involve a large number of consequences relating to additional education grants, maintenance grants for scholars, the need of Church schools, and so on. Some of these questions are so important that they would be considered by a Cabinet committee. No decisions could be reached without the same ample preparation. Others could be decided in the Department or by discussion with the Treasury. There might be questions about the school medical service to be discussed with the Ministry of Health. Questions relating to the release of scholars in special cases would be raised by or with the Ministry of Labour. In the Department itself somebody would have to consider the less important questions so as to instruct the draftsman. He in turn would raise points which seemed to him to need settlement one way or the other. There would be discussions with outside persons and bodies—perhaps the Archbishop of Canterbury, the leaders of nonconformity, the Association of Educational Committees, the National Union of Teachers, and so on. Memoranda would be prepared to form the basis of the minister's speeches: amendments would be examined and reasons given for not accepting them. Finally, when the Bill is passed, the administrative machinery must be set in motion. Regulations must be drafted, circulars sent out, forms designed, proposals from education authorities considered, difficulties discussed and overcome. In very little of all this would the minister take part. There is the same division of functions according to the importance of the issue.

§ 3. *Bureaucracy*

Accusations of "bureaucracy" usually relate to minor aspects of the process. It is said, for instance, that too wide powers can be exercised by the issue of Regulations. It is complained also that differences which ought to be submitted to the courts are handed over to "ministers" (which means "civil servants"). These are important complaints because they involve the rights and interests of individuals. They have been shown, nevertheless, to be based primarily on a misconception of modern administrative law. The State exercises new and wider functions which require quite a different technique of government from that suited to nineteenth-century conditions. The destruction of *laissez-faire* does not imply destruction of the methods used for the administration of private and criminal law, because the old functions remain and nothing suggests that the methods used for their execution were fundamentally wrong. These methods are not appropriate, however, for social insurance, planning, housing, and other twentieth-century functions.

The general problem caused by the growth of State functions is more important. In part it has been met by an increase in the number of Departments, and therefore of ministers; but this raises increased difficulties of co-ordination which are discussed in Chapter VII. In part it has been met by the creation of subordinate Departments. Experiments in this direction have not proceeded far, but, so far as they have gone, they have proved successful; and there is a strong case for the assertion that they might go further. The first effort was made in February 1916, when the Parliamentary Under-Secretary of State for Foreign Affairs was promoted to the Cabinet as Minister of Blockade. He remained subject to the general control of the Foreign Secretary, because the blockade involved questions of foreign policy, but he was free to take day-to-day decisions within the ambit of the Foreign Office policy. Also, by securing liaison with the Admiralty he was able to remove the many causes of friction which had developed between the two Departments in 1915.

The Ministry disappeared at the end of the war, but in the meantime the Department of Overseas Trade had been set up at the end of 1917. The reason for its establishment was the conflict of opinion between the Foreign Office and the Board of Trade as to who should control the commercial services, overseas-trade commissioners in the British Empire, commercial attachés in British legations, and consuls. Eventually it was decided to put the trade commissioners and the attachés under a new joint Department, though the consuls remained under the Commercial Department of the Foreign Office. The joint Department had at its head a Parliamentary Secretary, who was responsible both to the Foreign Secretary and to the President of the Board of Trade. As Under-Secretary of State for Foreign Affairs he also controlled, subject to the Foreign Secretary, the Commercial Department of the Foreign Office. The Government decided in 1928, as an economy measure, to abolish the Department. It nevertheless survives, and exercises substantially the functions for which it was set up in 1917, as well as functions under Export Credits schemes.

The third Department, the Mines Department of the Board of Trade,[1] was set up under a Parliamentary Secretary in 1920. The then President of the Board of Trade stated that the Parliamentary Secretary "should be in a position of complete responsibility so far as all the routine work of the Department is concerned, and

[1] There has also been a Petroleum Department of the Board of Trade since May 1940.

should only be responsible to the President of the Board of Trade in matters which really involve large policy". The proposal was criticised on the ground that ministerial responsibility would be "frittered away". "With that kind of divided responsibility", said Sir Leslie Scott, "the British Constitution will never work." During the past twenty years, nevertheless, the British Constitution has not broken down, and when it was proposed by the Government in 1928 to abolish the Mines Department and the Department of Overseas Trade, on grounds of economy, the criticisms were so severe that the proposal went no further. The system does not destroy ministerial responsibility, it makes it more effective; for the alternative is to allow decisions of substantial importance to be taken by civil servants. Far from being reprehensible, it provides a precedent which might be followed. It enables decisions of importance to be taken by ministers without increasing the number of separate Departments and thus aggravating the problems of co-ordination.

There is, however, one very real check which prevents delegation to civil servants from giving rise to bureaucracy. The responsibility of ministers to Parliament means that every decision, even if it is taken far down in the official hierarchy, may be criticised in Parliament. If a member considers that injustice has been done to an individual, or a wrong principle is being applied, he may ask the minister privately for an explanation. If he is not satisfied, or if he chooses not to use this method, he can ask a question in the House. If the answer does not meet his criticism, or if he thinks the subject important enough in any case, he may raise the subject in debate. By these means decisions are brought to the personal attention of ministers and, if they think that the criticisms have any value, they necessarily insist on Departmental investigation. Let us take a few examples at random. On 16 January 1940, the Secretary for Mines was asked about short-time in the pits of Lancashire, the Minister of Shipping about dry-dock accommodation at Newport, the Postmaster-General about licences for wireless sets in military camps, the Minister of Health about a pension for Mr C. F. Mott, and so on. It is possible that none of these matters had received ministerial attention before the questions were put down. Even if a minister gives a soothing answer, if there is any real difficulty there is a Departmental investigation.

Even more important than the fact that questions are asked is the fact that questions may be asked. The minister is compelled to deal with any matter which may be raised in Parliament. A civil servant is compelled to remember that his minister may get into a parliamentary wasps' nest if a decision proves to be unacceptable. The result is generally believed to be, not that the minister decides too little, but that he decides too much. Ministers must not make mistakes; therefore civil servants must not make mistakes. Consequently, it is complained that as compared with private enterprise a service like the Post Office is characterised by timidity. It tends to follow a routine, and where decisions have to be taken such care is shown and such caution exhibited that the whole question becomes wrapped in yards of "red tape". It is strange that many of those who make this accusation often make the accusation of what appears to be the opposite defect, that decisions are taken by "anonymous whipper-snappers" instead of by ministers. There is, of course, some truth in both complaints. It is inevitable that decisions should be taken by civil servants; it is also inevitable that some of them should tend to pass on their responsibility to their superiors, or to give such careful attention to a problem that a decision always comes too late.

There is no real harm in decisions being taken by civil servants. On the contrary, it is a waste of a minister's time to insist on his attention to a problem that raises no political issues. At the same time, it must be remembered that the line between political and administrative decisions is very fine. Moreover, even when the minister takes the decision or puts it before the Cabinet, the civil servants express their own views. It is not to be expected, nor is it to be desired, that officials of this calibre should not. The result is, however, that there is a "Departmental policy" independent of the minister and the Cabinet. It bows to political decisions, but it has profound effect on them. A minister who has no strong views of his own is almost certain to adopt the Departmental policy. A minister who has views of his own finds that, with the best will in the world, civil servants discover hosts of objections to his proposals when they conflict with their own ideas.

This "Departmental policy" must not be regarded as something formalised. It is not to be found expressed anywhere. It is certainly not a bureaucratic conspiracy. It is simply the product of the collective experience of the senior civil servants and of the bent of their minds. It has been possible to speak of "Treasury orthodoxy" in matters of finance. Indeed, we often hear references to the "Treasury mind". The Foreign Office was alleged to have francophil tendencies during the period when many people were profoundly suspicious of French foreign policy. The Colonial Office has been accused of Arab sympathies in relation to Palestine. It has been asserted that the India Office has been more sympathetic to Muslims than to Hindus, not for the reason given by the Congress politicians, that Great Britain desires to divide and rule, but because British administrators in India find Muslim culture more attractive than Hindu culture. It is not necessary to suggest that these assertions are true. They can never be proved because the evidence is necessarily too scanty. It is enough to point out that they can be made. It is assumed, in other words, that there is a Departmental policy which persists in spite of changing ministers and changing Governments.

Its importance must not be over-emphasised. No principle is more firmly fixed or more consistently carried out than the fundamental principle that ministers determine policy. When the Government decided in 1932 to turn its back on free trade, the Treasury officials at once put their minds to devising the best possible tariff system. Not all the pressure from white settlers in the colonies has been able to infringe the principle of the paramountcy of native interests. Mr Arthur Henderson, who was not accustomed to maintain amiable fictions for the sake of politeness, has borne witness to the spirit in which the Foreign Office assisted the change which he made in British foreign policy.

The system is nevertheless full of difficulties. Senior civil servants are able men, often more able than the ministers whose orders they take. Their arguments necessarily carry great weight. They would be failing in their duty if they did not frankly point out the difficulties which they foresee. Simple solutions attract politicians who do not see the ramifications of the consequences. It is the business of a Department to prevent a minister from making mistakes. Nevertheless, even the most expert may be wrong. No doubt it is possible now to give a verdict on the policy of "appeasement" which Mr Chamberlain and Lord Halifax carried in 1938. It was not so easy to do so in 1938. Assuming that the Foreign Office was against appeasement—there is little evidence, but it is a reasonable assumption—it is not easy to say precisely how emphatically they should have pointed out its dangers. Moreover, it is not merely a question of reaching a decision. Palmerston showed that, even when a policy has been adopted, it can be ruined by failure to put it into execution enthusiastically. To decide upon appeasement is not enough. Every step taken in foreign policy must be determined by that principle. If those who have the day-to-day responsibility of writing despatches believe that it is fallacious, they will necessarily act hesitatingly. It is certain that they would not try to sabotage a policy, as Palmerston did deliberately in 1851; but they would occasionally seek to minimise what appear to them to be the probable and undesirable consequences.

The allegation that Sir Robert Vansittart was "kicked upstairs" to the newly created office of Diplomatic Adviser and superseded as Permanent Under-Secretary of State because he agreed with Mr Eden and disagreed with Mr Chamberlain may not be true—he took a large part in the execution of the Munich policy as a member of the Foreign Policy Committee which was mis-named the Inner Cabinet. The fact that it could be plausibly maintained shows the existence of the belief that there may be occasions on which Departmental policy runs so emphatically counter to ministerial policy that a change of officials is necessary if the supremacy of ministerial policy is to be maintained. Similarly, it was alleged that that very able administrator Sir Evelyn Murray was transferred to the Board of Customs and Excise in 1934 because the views which he had formed during twenty years' service as Secretary to the Post Office were an obstacle to the reforms which Sir Kingsley Wood had decided to carry out.

How often problems of this kind arise it is impossible to say. They are capable of arising without reference to changes of Government. They might arise with even greater effect where policy was suddenly changed through a change of Government. Let us suppose that after the Entente Cordiale had been established in 1903 with the enthusiastic support of the Foreign Office, the new Liberal ministers had decided in 1905 that the policy was fundamentally wrong. Could we expect the same enthusiasm from the Foreign Office in carrying out the opposite? The position might be even more acute where a Labour Government succeeded a Conservative Government. The views which Sir Richard Hopkins of the Treasury laid before the Royal Commission on Unemployment Insurance in 1931 were emphatically condemned by many Labour politicians. The opinions which Sir Maurice Hankey stated to the Royal Commission on Armaments in 1935 ran directly counter to the Labour party policy. These were rare examples of the occasions on which civil service opinion becomes known. It is obvious, however, that many senior civil servants might be profoundly distrustful of Labour party policy. Few of them have personal experience or even knowledge of the segments of society which give the Labour party its ethos. They have been drawn almost entirely from university graduates of past generations—generations which knew not even the limited and highly selective scholarship system which now passes some persons of working-class origin into the administrative class. They have passed their official lives in working a system based essentially on private enterprise. They have lived, so to speak, between Whitehall and Wimbledon. It is reasonable to assume that the Treasury has none of the suspicions of the Bank of England exhibited at Labour party conferences. The Board of Trade may dislike the Mining Association, but it can hardly be unsympathetic to the eminent industrialists and leaders of commerce who from time to time give it assistance.

Again the problem must not be exaggerated. Criticisms which go so far as to suggest that there may be "sabotage" from the civil service are clearly ill-founded. The Labour ministers have given testimony to the assistance which they received between 1929 and 1931. It is true that they introduced no startling reforms; but the civil service tradition of political impartiality is so well-founded that any reforms would be carried out honestly. Moreover, previous discussions in this book have suggested that the argument that there is a fundamental opposition between the policies which a Conservative Government and a Labour Government would put into practice is ill-founded. Inevitability of gradualism implies not a fundamental change of policy but a change in the speed and, above all, the purpose of reform. Control over a public corporation involves but a slight extension of the peace-time control over private enterprise and hardly any extension of war-time control. Civil servants naturally believe that they are more efficient than ordinary business men; and the adoption of a policy of nationalisation is really a tribute to the civil service. Moreover, a change of policy in respect of industry is very different from a change of foreign or colonial policy. Nationalisation implies the setting up of an administrative system which civil servants, in their own interest, must work efficiently. A change in foreign policy, on the other hand, requires that the existing functions of the Foreign Office—in relation to the League of Nations, for instance—shall be carried on in a new spirit, and this is very difficult for a person who thinks the change to be wrong. The Secretary to a Coal Commission which controlled coal mines would necessarily try to make the working of the mines efficient. If the Permanent Under-Secretary of State thinks that the leaders of a foreign country are blackguards, it is not easy for him constantly to remember that, by a Cabinet decision, they have been made honorary gentlemen.

Nevertheless, it has been suggested by eminent Labour politicians—though not officially by the party— that it would be necessary to change the occupants of some of the key positions in order to make certain that full and enthusiastic collaboration was forthcoming. The admitted difficulties make it impossible to suggest that such action would be outrageous. It might, nevertheless, have dangerous consequences. If such officials were changed by a Labour Government and "sympathetic" officials promoted, it is reasonable to assume that a Conservative Government would feel compelled to do the same. If there were frequent changes of Government the result would be not only to cause frequent displacements in the higher ranks of the civil service, but also to place a premium on political "sympathy". The principle of political impartiality, which is one of the great benefits of the system of entry by examination, would thus be destroyed. Members of the administrative class would be associated with the political parties, and the "spoils" system would be on its way. In overcoming temporary inconvenience, a Labour Government would thus open a path to numerous abuses.

The problem needs to be attacked at an earlier stage. It is undesirable that civil servants should give evidence on their own account before Royal Commissions when questions impinging on politics are under examination. It would be preferable for ministers to appear; but if this is impracticable it should be made clear that statements represent the minister's opinion and not that of the civil servant. This is, however, to deal with the symptom and not with the cause. The criticism arises because it is felt that the senior civil servants are drawn from a single class and have, from their training, a narrow class sympathy. The solution lies in a more democratic educational system, in a more effective utilisation of promotion from the executive class, and in a wider system of post-entry training.

As a solution this has the defect of being slow in its operation, though ultimately it would be effective. In the meantime, and indeed at all times, a partial remedy lies in the hands of ministers. The problem arises only

n relation to a small minority of questions of political
mportance. It is for the minister to see that, in relation
to those questions, the advice goes no further than a fair
statement of the problem. If the case made is one-sided,
ve must insist that the other side be put. If the advice
enters into the political element, he must reject it because
ve alone is qualified to advise on political questions.
Frequently it will be found that there is a division of
opinion in the Department, and the greater use of
Departmental Committees, though taking more time,
nay be more effective than reliance on memoranda. Nor
should he accept the principle, which some permanent
heads of Departments desire to establish and maintain,
that all advice must pass through the Permanent Secretary. He is entitled to use the full resources of the
Department, to go direct to the technical experts, and to
consult whom he pleases. Nothing is more dangerous or
more destructive of initiative than the polite intimation
which is sometimes given to junior officials that it is not
their business to initiate policy. Finally, there should be
far greater use of outside expert opinion. In some degree,
this is being attained by the use of advisory committees,
though frequently these are badly composed. What the
minister really wants, however, is an independent report
from a person of knowledge and experience on the basis
of the information available in the Department as well as
outside. To do so it may be necessary to submit con-
fidential documents to outside expert opinion. There is
no great danger in such a process. It is an excellent
tradition of British public life that persons should be
prepared to place their knowledge at the disposal of the
State and to expect neither reward nor publicity.

CHAPTER VII

CABINET GOVERNMENT

§ 1. *Ministerial Responsibility*

The peculiar contribution of the British Constitution to political science is not so much representative government, which is an obvious solution, as responsible government. Added to representative government, it means that government is carried on by persons who are responsible to the representative House of the legislature, the House of Commons. Responsibility is secured by placing control of administration in the hands of politicians who are either members of or are represented by political subordinates in the House of Commons. So long as there is a House of Lords and ministers are unable to speak in both Houses, it is necessary that a few ministers should be in that House. As the law now stands, at least three ministerial heads of Departments, in addition to the Lord Chancellor, must be peers. This is not a very desirable arrangement, since neither the approval nor the disapproval of the House of Lords has much effect on Government policy, and the political issues are fought out in the House of Commons. Though it is not desirable that a person should be disqualified for ministerial office because he is a peer, he has considerable difficulty in exercising his main function through a subordinate minister in the House of Commons. Naturally, the peers like to have a few senior ministers in their own House, but the essential political

task is in the House of Commons. If the Foreign
Secretary is a peer, as in the case of Lord Halifax since
1938, the House of Commons is deprived of authorita-
tive expositions of foreign policy, because the Parliamentary Under-Secretary is a mere representative, and
an overworked Prime Minister cannot be familiar with
all aspects of policy. Moreover, the effective criticisms
of that policy are made in the House of Commons, where
the parliamentary opposition is to be found, and it is
necessary that the minister should be familiar with the
atmosphere in which criticism is made and that he
should be on the spot to defend himself. On the other
hand, to authorise ministers to speak in both Houses
would be to place a substantially increased burden on
their shoulders. That burden is already so great that it
should not be increased. The real solution is to insist
that all the heads of the great Departments should be
in the House of Commons, though it would require as
a corollary that peers should be capable of election to
the House of Commons.

The responsibility of ministers to the House of Commons is no fiction, though it is not so simple as it
sounds. All decisions of any consequence are taken by
ministers, either as such or as members of the Cabinet.
All decisions taken by civil servants are taken on behalf
of ministers and under their control. If the minister
chooses, as in the large Departments inevitably he must,
to leave decisions to civil servants, then he must take the
political consequences of any defect of administration,
any injustice to an individual, or any policy disapproved
by the House of Commons. He cannot defend himself
by blaming the civil servant. If the civil servant could
be criticised, he would require the means for defending
himself. If the minister could blame the civil servant,
then the civil servant would require the power to blame
the minister. In other words, the civil servant would

become a politician. The fundamental principle of our system of administration is, however, that the civil service should be impartial and, as far as may be possible, anonymous.

Complication arises from the fact that all decisions of real political importance are taken not by ministers as such but by the Cabinet. In normal times, the Cabinet contains all the heads of important Departments. The minister at the head of a Department is, so to speak, the representative of the Cabinet in relation to matters within the jurisdiction of his Department. Consequently, it is never very clear whether the minister is speaking as head of the Department or as the spokesman of the Cabinet. The House is not informed of the distribution of responsibility between the minister and the Cabinet. Often the question is one which in practice is decided by the House of Commons itself. The importance of a question is in large degree a parliamentary matter. If unemployment insurance is refused to John Smith of Rotherham, it is reasonably certain that the Minister of Labour knows nothing about it. If, however, the honourable member for Rotherham takes up the matter, it is at once raised to ministerial rank and the minister has to look into the matter. If the whole Opposition takes up the question because it appears to be a gross example of ministerial neglect or political discrimination, then it is almost certain that the Cabinet will have to discuss the matter.

The Cabinet is said to be collectively responsible for the whole policy of the Government, whether it has been brought before the Cabinet or not. This principle assumes that defective administration by or under the control of any minister should be laid to the door not of the minister but of the Cabinet. In practice, however, the principle is never carried so far, because it rests with the Cabinet whether they shall accept or disown the

ministerial decision. If the Cabinet chooses to disown
the decision, then the minister alone will resign. If the
Cabinet chooses to accept the decision as its own (as
appears to have happened when Sir William Joynson-
Hicks announced the intention to make the franchise for
women the same as that for men), the Cabinet will
treat the matter as one of confidence in itself. This
choice is open even if the decision criticised was that of the
Cabinet itself. For instance, the Hoare-Laval agreement
of 1935 apparently had Cabinet sanction; but so great
was the popular reaction that the Baldwin Cabinet
(which was unusually timid before public opinion)
decided to repudiate it. Sir Samuel Hoare was therefore
allowed to make himself a scapegoat and to resign his
office of Foreign Secretary.

If a decision is supported by the Cabinet, the question
becomes one of confidence in the Government. The
whips are put on, and members must take the responsibility either of supporting the Government or of risking
their resignation or a dissolution of Parliament. In
practice, for reasons already given, the party majority
supports the Government. No majority Government in
recent years has really had cause to fear a parliamentary
defeat (not even the Chamberlain Government in May
1940). Accordingly, the decision of the Cabinet to
support a minister is really based not on possible parliamentary consequences, but on the effect which the
decision may have on public opinion. Mr Baldwin did
not fear defeat in the House of Commons of the Hoare-
Laval proposals. What he feared was that public
opinion was moving so definitely against the Government that his party might suffer defeat at the general
election of 1935. With very rare exceptions, all questions
in the House of Commons are matters of confidence;
and what really matters is not the support of the House
but the support of the people. Once again, therefore,

we find that vocal public opinion provides the fundamental test.

Ministerial responsibility to the House of Commons is thus the means of assuring that government is in tune with popular opinion. A responsible government cannot be a bureaucracy; and it is for that reason that emphasis is laid so strongly on the principle that for the decision of a civil servant some minister must be responsible. It is true that there have been many recent examples of bureaucratic instruments deliberately established in order to avoid ministerial responsibility. For instance, the Central Electricity Board is practically independent of the Ministry of Transport because it has the technical function of operating the electricity "grid", and it is thought that, its operations being purely technical, it should be run on "business" and not on political lines. The Assistance Board provides another example established for a different reason. It was thought that the discretion of granting unemployment assistance allowances should be completely divorced from political control. The principles upon which discretion was exercised, as set out in the Unemployment Assistance Regulations, should receive the approval of Parliament (though Parliament should have power only to accept or to reject, not to amend). It was also thought that the amount of money to be made available to the Board should be under parliamentary control. But it was desired that the administration of discretion in individual cases should be freed from political influences.

This second example exhibits a suspicion of Parliament which has never been justified. It may have been true that when the "means test" was imposed by local authorities the principles upon which they operated depended on their political opinions. There is no evidence, however, that they discriminated among recipients according to their politics. Still more certain is it that

Parliament could not be an instrument of political discrimination among individuals. That a Labour majority would favour higher rates and a more generous discretion than a Conservative majority is obvious; but there is nothing in the position of the Assistance Board which prevents the House from determining general policy. It must always be remembered that the decisions of the House are the decisions of the Government. The Government whips are put on, and the majority votes with the Government. If there were individual discrimination, therefore, the Government would be responsible; but nothing is more certain than that any Government which attempted to discriminate in this way would lose heavily at the next general election. There is no "corruption" in the wide sense in which that term is used in North America, because the electorate has been educated for a century in "clean politics". Any Opposition would be delighted to receive a single example that it could put on every hoarding and repeat in every election speech. In fact, therefore, the Assistance Board has been a complete failure as an "independent" institution. It is neither more nor less subject to political control than the Ministry of Labour would be, and the only result of its "independence" has been to create a fruitful source of inter-Departmental conflict. If anything goes wrong, the officials of the Assistance Board blame the officials of the Ministry of Labour, and the officials of the Ministry blame the officials of the Assistance Board. This result was inevitable, and those who knew a little about British constitutional history freely forecast it before the Board was set up.

It is also necessary to emphasise that ministerial responsibility means only that a politician must be able to answer in the House of Commons for every act of administration. Emphasis is necessary because "ministerial responsibility" has become a slogan which is regarded as being a reason in itself, and the reason behind it has been forgotten. When, for instance, proposals have been made for vesting minor decisions in Parliamentary Secretaries, or for vesting major decisions in "Super-Ministers", the opponents have at once brought out the slogan. The fact that the Secretary for Mines answers for matters within his Department instead of the President of the Board of Trade does not infringe ministerial responsibility. On the contrary, it makes it more effective: for, if there were no Mines Department, there would be a Mines sub-Department. In other words, decisions at present taken by a junior minister would be taken not by the President of the Board of Trade but by the Principal Assistant Secretary at the head of the sub-Department. The House would be able to question the President of the Board of Trade, but the effective decision would be taken by a civil servant. The result of creating the Mines Department was that Parliament could criticise a minister who in all probability had himself taken the decision. Similarly, the fact that Mr Churchill is at present Minister of Defence does not detract from ministerial responsibility but increases its efficacy. Instead of asking three separate ministers to answer for the major problems of the co-ordination of defence, the House can ask the Prime Minister, who has had them under consideration. The effect of placing major responsibility in the Prime Minister as Minister of Defence has, in addition, enabled the three ministers in charge of the Defence Forces to control administration in more detail. They can thus answer more questions on the basis of their own knowledge. Ministerial responsibility does not mean undivided responsibility—it is always shared at least between the minister and the Cabinet; it means only political responsibility. The more ministerial responsibility is divided by adding to the number of ministers, the more effective the responsibility; though, of course, every new division adds to the problem of co-ordination.

§ 2. *The Cabinet*

The Cabinet can always have the last word. In peace time most of the items on its agenda are brought up from the Departments. In the normal process of government problems of a political order are met, new projects are considered, perhaps new legislation is required. Every Department concerned with the social and economic life of the country has in its pigeon-holes projects for reform which it is anxious to carry through when money and parliamentary time can be found. Even when there are no rampant dictators, questions of foreign policy have to be considered. Somewhere within the far-flung borders of the British Empire there are problems requiring immediate solution. No change or development of policy of any importance would be carried out without Cabinet sanction. If it required much money, the Treasury would certainly require prior Cabinet approval. If legislation were needed, the Cabinet must certainly decide upon it. In any other case the minister concerned would consider whether he could take the responsibility alone; and if he were in doubt he would consult the Prime Minister.

The Cabinet is also the court of appeal where two or more Departments differ about matters which affect them both or all of them. Administration does not fall neatly into twenty sections, in such a way that no dispute can exist as to the bounds of Departmental activity. Indeed, nearly every important problem cuts across Departmental boundaries. Even if no other Department is affected, the Treasury is almost certainly interested.

On purely inter-Departmental matters, the Departments would try to reach agreement. If they found themselves unable to agree, the Prime Minister might act as arbitrator and co-ordinator. In the last resort there must be appeal to the Cabinet. In fact, however, inter-Departmental questions are generally of a Cabinet order in any case.

Nor is there anything to prevent a minister from raising a question which does not affect his Department. The examples cannot be frequent, but they can be found. Joseph Chamberlain had opinions about most things. He did not think that his functions as President of the Board of Trade prevented him from discussing Home Rule with Parnell. Nor did he think that, as Colonial Secretary, he had nothing to do with social reform. Any minister may have views about foreign policy. Above all, the Prime Minister exercises a general oversight of the policy of the Government. He can no longer follow Peel's example and keep in touch with the work of every Department, but at least he must watch that ministers do not go joy-riding with Departmental policy.

Questions of this nature are, however, usually thrust upon the Cabinet by the logic of the political system. They are to be found in the party programme at the last election; or they are raised in the House of Commons; or they arise because some foreign power, or some section of opinion at home or in the Empire, takes action which makes them urgent. Foreign affairs are always the first item on the agenda, Foreign Office despatches are circulated daily, and, if some urgent question is raised, it is inevitable that the Cabinet should deal with it. Moreover, the House of Commons can raise any matter to Cabinet rank by making enough fuss about it. The Cabinet may prefer to let sleeping peers lie, but if a few members of the other House insist on debating the reform of the House of Lords, the Cabinet must decide either to do something or to do nothing. The Ministry of Labour may be entirely satisfied with the "means test", but the Opposition can keep the question on the Cabinet agenda. Here once more we meet that close relation between government and public opinion which needs to be stressed so often. Public opinion can rouse Parliament and Parliament can rouse the Cabinet. The Prime Minister determines the Cabinet agenda, but in large measure external forces determine what the Prime Minister shall place on it. Moreover, the Cabinet's primary concern is to keep itself in office, and its decisions must therefore keep pace with opinion.

In normal times the Cabinet meets for two hours each week during the session, and less frequently out of session. This is hardly more often than in the reign of Queen Anne. It is able to get through its business for several reasons. In accordance with the general tendency, more decisions are taken in the Departments, and the Cabinet dislikes having referred to it questions which are not of the first order. There is, too, better organisation of its work. Since the full Cabinet was restored in 1919 it has had a Secretariat, which produces an agenda under the Prime Minister's control and circulates documents where the Departments do not undertake to do so. The Cabinet usually insists on having a proposal documented, so that it can be considered beforehand and so that conclusions on it can be reached quickly. Moreover, it insists that no question shall be presented to it until it has been fully discussed between the Departments concerned. In other words, inter-Departmental discussions are conducted between the Departments or the ministers concerned, and do not take the form of cross-talk in the Cabinet unless it is impossible to reach agreement outside the Cabinet. The status of the Prime Minister, also, has so far advanced that, in consultation with the ministers, he can reach decisions which are not sufficiently important to be brought before the Cabinet. Finally, the Cabinet makes constant use of committees, both to reach substantially agreed proposals and to see that a decision reached in principle by the Cabinet is carried out in detail by the Departments.

The pressure upon ministers arises not from long and complex discussions in Cabinet, but from the numerous Departmental questions which they have to settle, from the burden of numerous committee meetings, from the increased demands of Parliament and of the party organisations, and above all from the variety and importance (rather than the number) of the decisions which have to be taken in Cabinet. By the time that a question reaches the Cabinet it has been reduced to first principles. The documents circulated are neither long nor numerous, particularly if we omit the Foreign office despatches, which are circulated for information and not for decision. Nevertheless, to decide such questions as those relating to German and Italian aggression, civil war in Spain, racial conflict in Palestine, Indian constitutional reform, discontent in Trinidad, rearmament, unemployment, spinsters' pensions, subsidies to farmers, the reorganisation of the cotton industry, the Highlands and Islands, and the rest, is no easy matter. A statesman's life is not a happy one. He has to determine issues of the most profound political and social significance on what must inevitably appear to him to be inadequate information. Necessarily he must rely upon the Departmental ministers and the Prime Minister. They, in turn, must lean heavily on their advisers. It is not work but worry that ages Cabinet ministers—though it has been said that some of them are an unconscionable time a-dying.

The nature of this task gives some indication of the qualities which ministers should possess. Obviously they must be of wide general understanding, capable of seizing quickly the essential points of a problem, and able to give a rapid decision. These qualities are essential for effective decisions, whether in the Department or in the Cabinet. They are included in that elusive but well-understood quality known as "judgment". Not all ministers possess it, and often it is the least prominent ministers who do, with the result that there are always members of the Cabinet whose presence is deemed essential by successive Prime Ministers, but whose qualities are rarely understood in the House of Commons. Among the most prominent ministers who appear to have had it during the past fifty years are Balfour, Campbell-Bannerman, Haldane, Baldwin, and Arthur Henderson. It must be emphasised, however, that sometimes it is possessed by the least prominent.

At least as important is such a knowledge of human nature as enables a minister to choose and rely on able assistants, whether ministers or civil servants. Judgment of this kind does not necessarily go with judgment in the realm of events. Of the statesmen mentioned above only Balfour and Arthur Henderson possessed both in any marked degree. Joseph Chamberlain and Lloyd George possessed judgment of men but were deficient in judgment of events. The quality of judging events, in fact, often goes with lack of initiative and imagination. This is not necessarily a defect. In a Prime Minister in peace time it is probably an advantage. In ordinary administration, when no serious problems have to be faced, the good administrator requires sound common sense rather than a fertile imagination. An imaginative minister is probably a volatile minister, like Lloyd George and the two Churchills. Gladstone was not exactly volatile, but he went too fast for his colleagues and his public—though not even 1886 and the last gasp of 1893 can deprive him of his pre-eminence.

Peel, the model Prime Minister, had no imagination. Joseph Chamberlain had not much imagination, but he had restless energy which caused more difficulty than all his qualities could offset. Disraeli's imagination fortunately spent itself in dreams, except in foreign and imperial policy, where it produced little wars and might have produced a big one. In war time, on the other hand, imagination and initiative are necessary. At such times the Salisburys, the Asquiths and (dare one say?) the Neville Chamberlains ought to be retired, unless they deliver the effective conduct of the war to the Disraelis, Joseph Chamberlains, Lloyd Georges and Winston Churchills.

"Judgment" usually makes a person a good committee man, and this is an essential quality. Yet persuasive committee men are sometimes deficient in judgment. Birkenhead was a little unstable, but an extremely good committee man. Kitchener was not only a bad administrator but a worse member of a committee, because he could neither make his own case nor answer the case put by another. Balfour, on the other hand, was extremely good.

Finally, it must be remembered that ministers are not only administrators but also politicians. They must be convincing in the House of Commons and persuasive in the country. These two qualities generally go together: yet sometimes they are distinct. Gladstone was extremely good both in Parliament and on the platform, but Disraeli was more at home in the House. Joseph Chamberlain was, in a very different way, an able debater and a good platform speaker. Many Labour politicians, however, fail in the House of Commons because their good platform technique is quite unsuited to the House. Ramsay MacDonald was, until about 1929, a political orator of the first class, but he was not effective in the House. The atmosphere is different, interruptions are more frequent, and they require answers, not appeals to the gallery. Peel, who was no orator, was very effective in the House, as even Disraeli admits. In these days, too, we must not forget the influence of the wireless. Baldwin was good and Snowden devastating. Readers can judge for themselves among His Majesty's present ministers. It is particularly important that the Prime Minister, in normal times, should have all the virtues, because his personality plays a large part in an election campaign. One can only ask what might have been the result in 1935 if Gladstone or Disraeli had led the Opposition.

The position of a Prime Minister is, however, peculiar, and it is considered more particularly hereafter. The question which we must now ask is whether the nation obtains the ministers that it requires. The primary consideration is that, except for a few peers, they are all drawn from the majority in the House of Commons. The quality of the ministers thus depends on the quality of the majority. Difficulties in this respect have already been mentioned. The standard of intelligence and ability in the House of Commons is higher than it is in the country generally, but it is not as high as it is in the administrative class of the civil service or in the top ranks of the professions or even—though this is more doubtful —among the ablest business men. The prizes of political ambition—power and prestige—are great, and they attract some of the ablest in the country: but it is always true that, outside a handful of members who "choose themselves" as ministers, almost any member would do equally well and equally badly.

Moreover, the choice rests with the Prime Minister. It is, of course, his business to choose a Cabinet which will work as a team, and to choose junior ministers who can work with their political superiors. Randolph Churchills, Harcourts and Joseph Chamberlains usually have to be appointed; but they, and others of the same kind though less able, can be a serious nuisance to the unity and the efficiency of a Cabinet. Where it is politically possible, such misfits have to be avoided. A weak Prime Minister, or a Prime Minister with little appreciation of human qualities, may nevertheless mistake criticism for obtrusive ambition or lack of team-spirit. Ramsay MacDonald was both weak and ignorant of men, and his efforts at team-making were extremely poor. They would have been worse if there had not been so many Labour members whose standing in the party compelled appointment. Where no such obstruction exists, such a Prime Minister is apt to choose colourless "yes-men". The path to political preferment passes through the field of party orthodoxy.

This situation is the more dangerous because, normally, ministers reach the Cabinet through junior offices. It is desirable that it should be so, because the House of Commons is generally a good judge of a minister, and one who does well as Parliamentary Secretary can usually be relied on to make a good Cabinet minister. If, however, junior ministers are members who have always voted straight, who have never opened their mouths except to bleat adulation, and whose title to promotion is that they have politely and unobtrusively carried messages as parliamentary private secretaries for some years, the more able but less compromising members never secure the training which will fit them for the Cabinet. The difficulty must not be exaggerated. The casual reader of newspapers need not be surprised that he knows the names of some private members and has never heard of half the Parliamentary Secretaries. The publicity-monger and the charlatan, the loud-mouthed and the gentleman of one idea, may secure a reputation outside Parliament when they have none in the Chamber. They supply "news" because they are obstreperous;

The first "National"
Government, 1931

and they are frequently obstreperous because they get their names in the papers. Nevertheless, there are in every Cabinet some ministers who surprise everybody except themselves that they have climbed so high. It is not that they are bad ministers, but only that they are very, very ordinary.

Nor must it be forgotten that Prime Ministers are no longer assiduous parliamentary listeners. They have far too much to do, and the Gladstonian tradition has gradually disappeared. In some degree the Prime Minister must rely on the whips, and the whips like members who speak when they are spoken to and vote when they are told. In other respects, he is apt to know of those who have famous names or have connections in Society. Austen Chamberlain did not get his first step up because of his qualities, substantial though they proved to be, but because he was the son of Joseph; and there have been much more flagrant examples.

The problem is not so acute as it might be, because the standard of the majority is usually high enough to produce a few leaders and a general competence among the other ministers. A Joseph Chamberlain thrusts himself into office, but the choice of *A* rather than of *B* usually makes very little difference. Moreover, it has been said already that the House is usually a good judge of a minister. Mere cleverness does not succeed, nor does mere oratory. What brought Gladstone to the front was not his roaring torrent of words, but his obvious grasp of the problems of trade and finance. Not all the social prestige nor all the arts of publicity can persuade the House that an eminent nincompoop knows his business. A Prime Minister is bound to choose the really able, and grumbling in the lobbies and criticism in the House prevents him from backing all his private fancies.

§ 3. *The Prime Minister*

The Prime Minister holds the key position in the British Constitution, and nearly all recent developments have tended to increase his authority. The extension of the franchise, added to the prestige which Gladstone and Disraeli conferred upon the office, have given him a status almost comparable with that of the President of the United States. A general election is in reality the election of a Prime Minister. The elector has a choice between Gladstone and Disraeli, Salisbury and Rosebery, Balfour and Campbell-Bannerman, Asquith and Balfour, Lloyd George and Asquith, Baldwin and MacDonald, MacDonald and Henderson, Chamberlain and Attlee. A party which has not a leader is in a hopeless position, and a party with a weak leader in a weak position. Indeed, in the Conservative party the leader is the party, for he controls the party organisation and is in command of its funds.

The support which he thus obtains is a party support, but it is a party support concentrated in the leader. The parliamentary majority is a party majority, but it owes allegiance to the leader, and it is spoken of as his majority. It is common to refer to his position in the Cabinet as *primus inter pares*; but this description is now far from being true. He chooses the ministers and determines which of them shall be in the Cabinet. It is true that certain of his prominent supporters choose themselves, but often he is in a position to ignore some of them. Mr Chamberlain could keep out Mr Churchill and Mr Amery, though Mr MacDonald could not keep out Mr Henderson. If he thinks fit, he can ask a minister to resign. He can shuffle his pack as he pleases. He alone determines whether and when Parliament shall be dissolved. It is extremely difficult to turn him out. The party majority must hold together, because if it does not it will probably put the Opposition into power. Some ministers may resign, as Mr Eden, Mr Duff Cooper and Mr Hore Belisha resigned after Mr Chamberlain came to office: but they are unlikely to desire to split the majority, and they can do no more than give more or less friendly advice, and more or less detached criticism, from below the gangway. A party which has a leader must usually bear with him; and if the Conservative party is in office, it is the King and not the party that chooses the leader.

It is true that the Prime Minister cannot exercise that oversight over Departmental business which Peel exercised. The functions of government are too vast. Nevertheless, he has what is called a "special responsibility" for the whole policy of the Government. Though the Labour party has consistently criticised the growing power of the office, it has done more than any to increase it. No doubt Mr Chamberlain took a more exaggerated view of his functions than any Prime Minister since Mr Lloyd George, and no doubt also the foreign policy which had been the most important branch of government since 1936 was his policy until it turned to dust in March 1939. Nevertheless, the Labour Opposition consistently followed the practice of charging Mr Chamberlain with all the alleged faults of his Government. There was a similar tendency under Mr Baldwin, but his alleged "laziness" (which consisted in large degree of leaving to Departmental ministers matters which were not of primary importance) prevented the practice from completely submerging the personalities of his ministers.

The office is necessarily what the holder chooses to make it and what the other ministers allow him to make of it. His powers are large, but he has to secure the collaboration of his colleagues. Neither Salisbury nor Balfour could (even if they had so desired) have prevented the limelight from falling on Joseph Chamberlain. On the other hand, not even he could take the centre of the stage while Gladstone was behind the footlights. Rosebery's Government descended to futility because the Prime Minister was not strong enough to control Harcourt. Campbell-Bannerman, on the other hand, increased his strength in the long years of desolate opposition until he became capable of managing even the strong team that took office in 1905.

The office really requires varied and quite inconsistent qualities. On the one hand, the Prime Minister as party leader must have a strong personality, capable of dominating the political scene and inspiring confidence in a suspicious electorate. The issue before the country while Gladstone was alive, even when he was not leader of the Liberal party (as in 1880), was not whether there should be a Liberal Government, but whether he should be Prime Minister. None of his successors has occupied such a position, though Lloyd George approached it in 1918. On the other hand, what is wanted in the Cabinet is not a dominating personality but a good chairman. Gladstone was not a good chairman because he tended to be the whole committee. He always had a policy of his own, and therefore tended to concentrate on some aspects of government instead of supervising the whole. If he had been less concerned with his pet projects, he would not have allowed Gordon to be sent to Khartoum; if Gordon had been appointed, he would not have let him die through disobeying orders. It is true that Gladstone made few mistakes of this order, but the example shows the danger. Indeed, a Prime Minister in peace time ought not to have a policy. If he has able ministers, he ought to rely on them, and policies should come from Departmental ministers, assisted as they are by all the knowledge and experience that their Departments can offer. The qualities which made Lloyd George a great Prime Minister in war time made him a disastrous Prime Minister in peace time, when Curzon at the Foreign Office was "almost an Under-Secretary". Salisbury would have been a better Prime Minister if he had not also been Foreign Secretary—and perhaps there would have been no Boer War. The reader can judge for himself whether Mr Neville Chamberlain's "appeasement" policy was a success.

The best chairmen have in fact been those who had the least popular appeal. Sir Austen Chamberlain—who served under five Prime Ministers from Balfour to MacDonald—once told the present writer that the best of them was Balfour, and there is other evidence to the same effect. Balfour's reputation has suffered because he had an impossible task even while Joseph Chamberlain was in the Cabinet pressing tariff reform; it became impossible after Chamberlain was let loose in 1903. Moreover, he was Prime Minister of a Government which had snatched a huge majority out of the apparent end of the Boer War. Even if the tariff reformers had not assisted its decline and fall, it would certainly have been heavily defeated in 1905. What Sir Austen Chamberlain meant was that Balfour was superb at keeping a discussion to questions of principle and drawing a conclusion out of it if a conclusion was to be reached. The difference between Balfour and Gladstone was the difference between a driver who keeps his team going hard even when they want to bite each other, and a driver who lets his team loose and pulls the carriage himself.

Nor are the Prime Minister's conciliating and encouraging functions limited to the Cabinet. A minister needs an experienced political adviser whom he can consult. Balfour was prepared to listen, consider, and advise. Baldwin was prepared to listen, but generally let the minister decide for himself. MacDonald was not prepared to listen and was incapable of advising. Lloyd George wanted to do all the talking. Moreover, if the Prime Minister is to keep control and to exercise properly his Cabinet function of leading the discussion to a conclusion, he must not only be ready for consultation, he must also take the initiative. MacDonald realised the need for informing himself, but he had a dislike of most of his colleagues, including Snowden and Henderson, and he was hardly on speaking terms with them. He tried, therefore, to compensate by reading endless documents. As a chairman he was fully informed, but there was not that confidence between Prime Minister and colleagues which makes for effective decisions.

The position is quite different in war time because then one aspect of policy (though it has many facets) dominates the whole political scene. A Prime Minister with a policy, or capable of forming one by consultation, is therefore desirable. He thus requires a forceful personality, capable of securing rapid and effective action. He ceases to be a mere chairman or co-ordinator and becomes chief of a vast war machine. He is, in other words, no longer chairman of the board of directors of a holding company, but managing director of an even larger operating company. It is therefore obvious that the qualities required are quite different. Pitt was no great success even in the conduct of what, in the eighteenth century, was called "war". Peel would probably have been a failure because, though a great administrator, he took years to assimilate a new idea. Gladstone would have been a great war minister and Disraeli even a greater, provided that he had had subordinates who paid attention to detail. Campbell-Bannerman and Balfour would have been quite ineffective, while Joseph Chamberlain would have been excellent. Asquith was poor, even before his son's death, while Lloyd George was a success.

§ 4. *Co-ordination*

Peel's Cabinet of 1841 contained fourteen ministers; but of these five had no serious Departmental duties. Outside the Cabinet were five ministerial heads of Departments; but of these only the Chief Secretary for Ireland, the Postmaster-General and (perhaps) the Chief Commissioner of Land Revenue, had real Departmental duties. Thus, the Prime Minister and the Cabinet had to co-ordinate the activities of at most twelve Departments. Moreover, each of these Departments had much less work to do than is now the case. It has also to be remembered that, while the Government had Ireland on its hands, in other respects the range of its interests was smaller. India was governed by the East India Company, and the function of the President of the Board of Control, who was in the Cabinet, was primarily to act as liaison between the Government and the Company. Also, the Army was governed from the Horse Guards, and the functions of the Secretary at War, who was in the Cabinet, were primarily financial. Complete control over the Army was not taken until 1895. Since Departmental work was much smaller, ministers could decide a high proportion of Departmental questions; and since the functions of government were fewer, the Cabinet could decide every problem of any importance.

In 1936 (that is, before the expansion necessitated by the approach of war), the Cabinet contained twenty-one ministers, of whom five (the Prime Minister, the Lord Chancellor, the Lord President of the Council, the Lord Privy Seal, and the Minister for the Co-ordination of Defence) had no serious Departmental duties. Outside the Cabinet were six ministerial heads of Departments, of whom the Minister of Transport, the Minister of Pensions and the Postmaster-General had substantial

Departmental duties. The changes since 1841 included the disappearance of the Chief Secretary for Ireland; the substitution of the Secretary of State for War for the Secretary at War, of the Secretary of State for India for the President of the Board of Control, and of the Minister of Agriculture and Fisheries for the First Commissioner of Land Revenue; and the addition of the Secretary of State for the Dominions, the Secretary of State for Air, the Secretary of State for Scotland, the Minister for the Co-ordination of Defence, the President of the Board of Education, the Minister of Health, the Minister of Labour, the Minister of Transport, and the Minister of Pensions. The increase of work within the Departments has already been emphasised.

If for the time being we use the term "Departmental ministers" to cover only those who have substantial functions as heads of Departments, the change may be expressed by saying that the number of such ministers had increased from twelve to twenty-one. Some of the new Departments had the heaviest duties to perform, since they included the Air Ministry, the Board of Education, the Ministry of Health, the Ministry of Labour and the Ministry of Transport. The number of civil servants had increased from 40,000 to 500,000 and the national expenditure from £50,000,000 to £1,000,000,000. By June 1940 the number of "Departmental ministers" had increased to twenty-seven, the Ministries of Supply, Food, Information, Economic Warfare, Shipping and Aircraft Production having been created. No mention has been made of the Burma Office and the Ministry of Home Security because they remain under ministers holding other offices. The expenditure forecast in the first Budget of 1940 was £2,000,000,000.

The functions of government do not fall nicely and conveniently into twenty-one or twenty-seven sections. The actions of one Department may require the collaboration of several more. It is easy to find examples. The landing of troops in Norway and the withdrawal from Dunkirk required the intimate collaboration of the Admiralty, the War Office and the Air Ministry. It required also money from the Treasury, ships from the Ministry of Shipping, transport within Great Britain from the Ministry of Transport, equipment from the Ministry of Supply, and food from the Ministry of Food. Such collaboration is needed, also, not only at the moment of decision and afterwards, but long before. Nobody had, before the war, contemplated that British troops might be landed in Norway; but in the preparation for the event of war it was necessary to assume that an expeditionary force might have to be landed somewhere under the eyes of the enemy, and to make skeleton plans accordingly.

Another example may be drawn from the supply of food to the civilian population in war time. Distribution is the business of the Ministry of Food, but production in Great Britain is controlled by the Ministry of Agriculture and Fisheries and transport by the Ministry of Transport. The Ministry of Shipping must see that ships are available to bring supplies from overseas and the Admiralty and the Air Ministry that they are convoyed. Nobody can do anything unless the Treasury finds the money. Transport requires coal and petrol, controlled by the Mines Department and the Petroleum Department respectively. Foreign trade is the business of the Board of Trade, but it involves wider aspects of foreign policy which are within the jurisdiction of the Foreign Office. Much of our supply comes, however, from the British Empire overseas, so that the Dominions Office, the Colonial Office, and the India and Burma Offices are necessarily concerned.

These are war-time examples, though they involve the preparation of plans in time of peace. Nevertheless, the problems of peace are hardly less complicated. Our economic problems involve the collaboration of practically all the Departments. Consider, for instance, the question of a duty on imported wheat. This is primarily the responsibility of the Treasury, but it involves questions of foreign trade which are the concern of the Board of Trade. The internal consequences depend upon the supply of home-grown wheat, with which the Ministry of Agriculture and Fisheries is concerned. If there were a rise in the cost of living, the Ministry of Labour would have something to say. That increase might require an increase in national health insurance benefits, contributory pensions, and public assistance, so that the Ministry of Health would have comments to make. Nor could duties be imposed on wheat without affecting our relations with the Dominions and foreign countries.

These are questions of a Cabinet order, but they require collaboration between Departments before they reach the Cabinet and further collaboration in the execution of Cabinet decisions. Such collaboration is necessary, however, in respect of matters which never reach the Cabinet. Suppose, for instance, that a local authority submits to the Ministry of Health a planning scheme which, among other things, schedules certain areas for industrial development and certain other areas as "mainly agriculture", and which provides lines for new roads. It is obvious that if the plan were properly considered it would be examined by the Ministries of Labour, Agriculture, and Transport as well as by the Ministry of Health. Probably, it will be considered by the Ministries of Health and Transport alone; but the example merely shows that co-ordination is not adequate. Actually, other Departments also are concerned in planning. If a new industrial estate or garden city were contemplated, new schools and post offices would be required and gas and electricity services extended, apart from the matters which are under the control of the Ministry of Health. These examples, it must be pointed out, relate to questions which would probably never go to a minister at all.

Co-ordination is one of those magic phrases which are apt to be on everyone's lips but which few care to take the trouble to define. For instance, in a debate on economic co-ordination on 1 February 1940, the Government's critics were considering different aspects of the problem. Mr Chamberlain thought that he was answering them when he pointed out that they were asking for different things, though in fact he was merely demonstrating that co-ordination was lacking on several different levels of administration. Co-ordination machinery is designed to fulfil several different functions and, though they are closely connected, it is wise to take them separately.

(1) *Overlapping of Powers*

Theoretically, each Department should be doing different things. Two Departments ought not to be in a position to give contradictory orders, nor should it be necessary for an individual outside to approach two Ministries to obtain permission to do a certain act. In practice, it is very difficult to separate powers precisely. For instance, the Ministry of Health is concerned with planning; but planning involves the planning of roads, and the Ministry of Transport is concerned with roads. Again, the Ministry of Agriculture is concerned with food production; but food is produced for distribution and the Ministry of Food is concerned with food distribution.

There is far more involved in these examples than a question of overlapping of powers, but they show how necessary it is to define the powers closely in the first instance. Theoretically, this particular problem is not difficult. In peace time powers are conferred by legislation which is approved by the Cabinet. The Cabinet is thus expected to prevent overlapping. In war time, however, the powers are taken by delegated legislation —by Orders in Council under the Emergency Powers (Defence) Acts or by rules under Regulation 55 of the Defence Regulations, 1939, which in turn was an Order in Council issued under the Acts. Something like 2500 Orders and Rules have been issued in less than twelve months. Possibly they have all gone to the Cabinet, but it is extremely unlikely that they have all been read by any single person whose function it is to see that powers are precise and distinct.

(2) *Encroachment*

Even if powers appear to be distinct and without overlapping, they must be expressed in general language. They are interpreted, however, by the Departments themselves. "Under S.R. & O., 1939, No. 2000," a Department may say, "we have power to stop so-and-so from doing this sort of thing." It is possible, however, that "so-and-so" has already approached another Department and has received permission to do what he wants to do, under, say, S.R. & O., 1939, No. 2005. It may be that the two Orders are quite distinct in their terms but are capable of being interpreted so as to give one Department power to prevent and another Department power to permit. It is easy to conceive of confusion in this respect between the powers over wheat production possessed by the Ministry of Agriculture and the powers over flour milling possessed by the Ministry of Food.

If he thought fit, "so-and-so" could challenge before the courts the validity of the former Department's refusal; but no one likes litigating against a Government Department, and indeed only a wealthy corporation with much at stake would run the risk of being taken from the High Court to the Court of Appeal, and perhaps to the House of Lords. In any case, these august bodies may not have completed their deliberations before the war is over; and certainly the harvest will have come and gone.

(3) *Duplication*

The example given in the previous paragraphs might have been a perfectly proper exercise of quite distinct powers. The one Department might have given permission because, so far as it was concerned, there was no objection; the other might have refused because, so far as it was concerned, there was objection. The reason would be that the problem had to be considered in two aspects, and "so-and-so" ought to have applied to both. For instance, if Jones wishes to build a house by the side of a main road in an area for which a town-planning resolution is in existence, he would have to apply for permission to both the county council and the district council. If both refused, he would need to appeal both to the Ministry of Transport and to the Ministry of Health. The former might allow the appeal because, from the angle of road safety, there was no objection; the latter might reject the appeal because the building would be unsightly or would interrupt the view, or would demand unnecessary extension of water mains and sewers. "Ribbon development" is not a problem of road safety alone; it is, in addition, a problem of uneconomic health services. It is, therefore, the concern of two Ministries.

Examples of inevitable duplication of this kind are numerous. For instance, the Board of Education is concerned with the health of school children because empty stomachs mean empty heads and bad eyes or bad teeth mean bad education. School children are, however, part of the ordinary population whose health is the concern of the Ministry of Health. Moreover, the children may be starved or diseased because their fathers are unemployed and are receiving insufficient assistance from the Assistance Board, whose scales are the concern of the Ministry of Labour. We could, in fact, start another line of connections, showing that the Ministry of Food was to blame because it was allowing prices to rise; the Ministry of Food would blame the Ministry of Shipping, the Ministry of Shipping would blame the Treasury, and so on.

The point here is, however, that two Departments may be concerned with an application from the same person to do a single act because that act has two aspects. It would be much simpler, cheaper and more expeditious if he could make one application and leave the two Departments to settle the question in respect of both of its aspects. For instance, it is unnecessary for an application for ribbon development to be considered by two inspectors at different sittings, involving two arguments by lawyers, two sets of costs, two payments for the hire of rooms, and so on.

This kind of duplication is obvious to persons outside the Government service, but there may be other examples not so obvious. For instance, the Foreign Office requires information about public opinion overseas. For this purpose it has representatives overseas who telegraph summaries of newspaper opinion. It has also an organisation based on the Royal Institute of International Affairs (Chatham House), which summarises newspaper opinion. The prevention of overlapping is an internal question for the Foreign Office. The Ministry of Information, however, must have information about public opinion in neutral countries if its operations are to be successfully conducted. It would be wasteful to have one "Chatham House" for the Foreign Office and another for the Ministry of Information. The B.B.C. has a foreign news service which similarly must take account of foreign opinion. Clearly, there ought not to be yet another "Chatham House" for the B.B.C.

(4) Competition

The Departments are large purchasers of commodities, especially in war time. Except where the commodities are requisitioned, they compete in the open market. This may mean that they compete with each other. For instance, the Army, the Navy, the Air Force, the Post Office, the Office of Works, the Ministry of Transport, and many more, all require motor vehicles. The three Defence Services (which, in the case of the Army, means the Ministry of Supply) require machine guns, ammunition, food, fuel, huts, and so on. It would be wasteful and ridiculous for Government Departments to bid against each other. Moreover, it is not only a question of preventing competition. If, for instance, the Royal Marines and the Army used different kinds of rifles, costs would be put up because manufacturers would have to follow different designs for the provision of the rifles themselves and all their parts, and also for the provision of ammunition. Stocks available for the one would not be available for the other.

Again, there may be competition for man-power as well as competition for commodities. Not only might there be competition among the Defence Services, but also a competition between the Services and other Departments. One of the weakest points of our organisation in 1914–18 was that the Army was using for the front line, or for fatigue duties, skilled men who were urgently required at home.

(5) The Application of Inconsistent Principles

"Policy" is usually said to be a matter for the Cabinet. It has already been pointed out, however, that there is a policy at each level of administration. The

Cabinet decides policy in very general terms. For instance, the Cabinet may decide that two new battle-ships shall be built, at a cost estimated by the Treasury and the Admiralty in consultation at £20,000,000. If the Treasury and the Admiralty had agreed on a cost of £19,500,000 or £20,500,000, however, the Cabinet would have agreed as readily. The difference of £500,000 is not a Cabinet question unless the two Departments disagree. There is, nevertheless, a policy involved in the £500,000, which is regarded by the Cabinet as an inter-Depart-mental matter so long as the Departments are agreed. Having obtained Cabinet sanction for £20,000,000, the Admiralty proceeds to elaborate plans (though in fact the outline will be clear already because it was necessary to make a rough plan in order to estimate the cost). If the Board of Admiralty decides to build one costing £10,500,000 and another costing £9,500,000, it is un-likely that the Treasury will raise objections: this is a purely Departmental question. Further, the armament to be provided is the concern of the Board of Admiralty; but within the lines which they decide upon the Fourth Sea Lord would have wide discretion. Moreover, though the Fourth Sea Lord would approve the terms of the contracts, there is plenty of scope for discretion by his junior officers.

The fact is that wherever there is a discretion there may be a policy. If there is not, there ought to be, because decisions ought not to be taken except in terms of some consistent principle. Discretionary powers are exercised at least as far down in the civil service as the Assistant Secretaries and frequently much further. Where different Departments are dealing with cognate sub-jects, however, the principles applied in the exercise of discretionary powers are quite likely to conflict. This is especially clear in economic matters, since a nation's economy is a unit and, indeed, is merely part of world economy. The details of a commercial agreement with Spain, for instance, will be the concern of officials in the Treasury, the Board of Trade, the Ministry of Economic Warfare, the Ministry of Supply, the Ministry of Food, the Ministry of Shipping, and perhaps the Foreign Office. Again, propaganda in the Balkans is a matter of detail, but it involves collaboration between the Ministry of Information, the Foreign Office, and the B.B.C. The stopping of supplies to Germany through neutrals is the direct concern of the Royal Navy—and this may mean the exercise of a discretion by the commanding officer of a single destroyer—but the instructions come from the Ministry of Economic Warfare. Those instructions may, however, raise difficulties with neutral powers and so come within the province of the Foreign Office; or with a Dominion, and so come within the province of the Dominions Office; or with India, and so come within the province of the India Office.

The Defence Services, however, provide the most obvious examples. The Air Force and the Navy assist the Army, the Army assists the Air Force and Civil Defence. The Air Force assists the Navy. This means that at every stage of administration, from the Cabinet down to the individual company, squadron or ship, there may be need of collaboration. If at any stage there is inconsistency in the principles adopted, there may be confusion, loss of life, or an enemy success.

(6) *Major Policy*

The major principles of policy are determined by the Cabinet. Here, it would seem, there is co-ordination and no need to discuss the point further. It is, however, just at this fundamentally important stage that co-ordination may be weakest. The need for co-ordination of the kind illustrated above has been realised, whereas even Cabinet ministers have failed to realise that often it is in their own activity that the system is weakest. Careful examination of Mr Chamberlain's speech on economic co-ordination on 1 February 1940 reveals that he was thinking in terms of inter-Departmental disputes. He gave a long account of the many devices used to settle these problems. He did not meet the criticism of the Opposition because they were thinking in terms of major policy. His view of co-ordination was arbitration between Departments; their view of co-ordination was the formulation of economic policies which needed execution by several Departments. The criticism was summarised in the statement of *The Economist*[1] that "the Government have no apparent policy on prices, wages, labour mobilisation, exports or finance": or, in other words, each Department was left to decide without an overriding Cabinet policy.

Proposals on major policy come to the Cabinet from two sources. First, they may be brought up by Cabinet ministers themselves and be derived, so to speak, from the ministers' own heads. Most ministers are not noted for original ideas, and few of them have time to think. Indeed, when a minister was appointed during the depression to exercise the function which caused him to be called "Minister for Thought" he found that he had so little to do that he resigned. Nevertheless, many ideas come in through ministers' heads even if they do not originate there. Criticism in the press, and still more often in Parliament, is accompanied by suggestions, often futile but occasionally fruitful, as to the policy to be pursued. If an obscure professor has an idea, for instance, he does not approach a minister. If he has a friend in the relevant Department, he may develop it over luncheon—though this method has the disadvantage that the friend is probably not authorised to make suggestions on this line of policy and can make it

[1] Vol. 138, p. 133.

effectively only by having another friend to luncheon. Alternatively, the professor may write a memorandum for a member of Parliament and hope that the member will "catch the Speaker's eye" at one of those rare moments when a Cabinet minister is listening, that the member will not bowdlerise the suggestion, and that the Cabinet minister will understand it and will remember it if he does. Much the best plan, however, is to write an article for some journal of opinion, where it will be read by civil servants, by members of Parliament looking for material for speeches, by other journalists looking for material to write about, or even by Cabinet ministers. This last process is slow, but, if the idea is a good one, usually effective, because a "public opinion" is created.

In fact, however, ideas rarely become policies by this route. It is a long and exhausting journey, as the history of any great policy—like franchise reform, the repeal of the Corn Laws, Home Rule, or even the League of Nations—shows. More often, the policy comes from a Department. More often than not, of course, the policy comes to the Department from outside. Civil servants are even busier than ministers, and the Treasury does not approve of people who sit and think because it fears (perhaps rightly) that they are more likely just to sit. However, the Departments have in recent years experimented with advisory committees, and even with Economic, Industrial and Diplomatic Advisers, and policies are often based on special investigations by Royal Commissions, Departmental Committees, and the rest.

In war time the gap between proposal and execution must be small if government is to be effective. The difficulty of securing rapid and effective action is that government is compartmentalised, and proposals must normally come from separate Departments. Each Department considers ways and means to make its own administration more effective, but major policies require concurrent action by many Departments. A policy proposed by the Ministry of Economic Warfare, for instance, may require both for its formulation and for its execution the co-operation of the Treasury, the Board of Trade, the Admiralty, the Ministry of Shipping, the Ministry of Food, the Ministry of Agriculture, the Ministry of Transport, and so on.

Let us suppose that X, an Assistant Secretary in the Ministry of Economic Warfare, has a bright idea. He gets his assistants to work it out in the form of a memorandum. He then puts it before his immediate superior, who consults the minister. It then goes to the Treasury, where it goes down to an Assistant Secretary and up again, with the result that "My Lords" do not disapprove. It involves, however, the collaboration of six other Departments, and so it goes to six ministers to go down to six Assistant Secretaries (at least) and up again. "It" is perhaps the wrong word, for by this time it is probably not a memorandum but a bulging file of memoranda and minutes. So, at last, the prodigal son comes home again and his father the Assistant Secretary makes a memorandum for the War Cabinet and a "brief" for his minister. Assuming that there are no further delays, the War Cabinet at last decides on major policy.

Possibly the hypothetical case is exaggerated. It is, however, strictly in accord with peace-time practice. Indeed, there is very good reason in it. Normally the congestion is at the top, and it is essential that a question should not come to the Cabinet until it has been fully examined in all the Departments likely to have views on it. If a "half-baked" proposal comes from a Department, there will be debates in Cabinet and in Cabinet committees which will occupy much of the valuable time of ministers. Accordingly, Cabinet instructions since 1931 have laid down the rule that memoranda are not to be circulated until their subject-matter has been fully examined between the Department from which they emanate, the Treasury, and other Departments concerned.

In peace time, such proposals generally affect only two or three Departments besides the Treasury, and substance is more important than time. In war time, however, many more Departments are often concerned, because this is a totalitarian war, waged with all the resources of the nation; and time is of the essence. Further, it is by no means certain that Departmental initiative is necessarily the right method. New weapons of warfare do not mean only tanks, magnetic mines, and the rest (though the failure to develop the tank and to use it properly was a notable example of lack of co-ordination in the last war); they include economic and propaganda weapons. The Departments are concerned primarily with their existing technique. They make valuable suggestions for its alteration and development. They can hardly be expected to develop revolutionary methods. Nor is it even possible for a Department to think of a particular problem as a whole. Price policy raises issues affecting the Treasury, the Board of Trade, the Ministry of Agriculture, the Ministry of Food, the Ministry of Transport, the Ministry of Supply, the Ministry of Economic Warfare, the Ministry of Labour, and even the Ministry of Health (e.g. in respect of pensions and national health insurance). We cannot expect any official in any of these Departments to produce for his Minister, and the Minister to produce to the Cabinet, a policy which takes into account all the many facets of this most complicated problem.

In other words, we are here faced with the most difficult problem of co-ordination, the formulation of major policy in such a manner that sound and rapid

decisions can be taken by the War Cabinet. Attempts
have been made to solve it, as attempts have been made
to solve the other problems mentioned in this Chapter.
Whether they have been wholly successful, or can be
successful with the existing machinery, is part of the
issue to be raised.

§ 5. *Instruments of Co-ordination*

It must not be thought that the problem of co-
ordination always requires a special institution for its
solution. The most important method is that which is
purely informal, the day-to-day collaboration between
Departments, secured by personal interview and by
correspondence. Particularly is this true of the Treasury,
whose relations with other Departments are necessarily
close. The chief financial officer in a Department is
appointed by the Prime Minister, acting on the advice
of the Permanent Secretary to the Treasury; and though
he is a Departmental officer he is also the "watch-dog"
of the Treasury. He points out to the official concerned
with action involving expenditure that the Treasury
must be consulted at some stage, and the sooner the
better. Close contact is therefore maintained with the
Treasury long before any formal submission is made for
the consent of "My Lords". This informal collaboration
is, however, only an example of a daily occurrence. No
civil servant likes a "row", and he knows that, whereas
any other Department concerned is likely to prove
"sticky" if proposals for action are developed without
consultation, it will probably give what assistance it can
if it is consulted at an early stage. If informal consulta-
tions are likely to take long, or if a dispute does arise,
the simplest procedure is to appoint *ad hoc* an inter-
Departmental committee to settle the principles involved and the boundaries of Departmental jurisdiction.

These methods assume that from the beginning the one Department realises that the other may be affected. This is not necessarily so, because the official, running along his own tramlines, may not realise that before he gets to the end of his journey he will reach a junction. Disputes and delay may occur if he has suddenly to put on the brakes. Accordingly, officials are often seconded for service in other Departments as liaison officers, so that they may draw attention to matters affecting the Departments to which they belong. This method is of special use in war time, when delays would be dangerous.

In other cases a more formal organisation is necessary. It has already been mentioned that the Department of Overseas Trade was set up as a joint Department of the Foreign Office and the Board of Trade because agreement could not be reached as to which Department should control commercial attaches and consuls. The Ministry of Health and the Board of Education employ the same person as Chief Medical Officer, so that there shall be no confusion between the general medical service and the school medical service. The Colonial Office and the Dominions Office, the India Office and the Burma Office, and the Home Office and the Ministry of Home Security, use the same executive and clerical staff. On minor questions joint standing committees are frequently set up.

These examples relate entirely to the lower levels of administrative discretion—to "Departmental policy". The need for co-ordination at a higher level has only recently been recognised because the Cabinet and the Prime Minister are supposed to co-ordinate high policy. In large measure they do; it must be remembered, however, that policies are rarely initiated by the Prime Minister or in the Cabinet. The Prime Minister is an extremely busy person, with little time for original thought. Indeed, it has already been suggested that, in normal times and apart from his capacity as party leader, a good Prime Minister is a good chairman of committees. He ought to be, and usually is, an excellent arbitrator. He can decide and ought to decide Departmental disputes which cannot be settled between the contesting Departments. He ought not only to be available to Ministers when they find themselves at cross-purposes, he ought also to have enough knowledge of what goes on in the Departments to realise when conditions are becoming "sticky". He should be able to intervene when action is being held up by difference of opinion, to provide a new demarcation of functions where it can be done without raising questions of principle or demanding legislation, and to shuffle or remove ministers where personal differences stand in the way of effective collaboration. Subject to an exception to be mentioned presently, he has no machinery for developing policy, and though sometimes he may be able to make suggestions as to questions that might be fruitful, he is unlikely to have information adequate enough to permit him to override a Department unless some other Department agrees with him. In other words, he is not in a position to achieve collaboration where co-ordination is most required—in the planning of Government policy as a whole—though he can be a most efficient judge of Departmental differences. So much is this so that some Prime Ministers—Mr Baldwin and Mr Chamberlain, for example—have thought that when demands have been made for better co-ordination they were implicitly a criticism of the Prime Minister. Mr Baldwin thought that the function of a Minister for the Co-ordination of Defence was the settlement of disputes between the Chiefs of Staff; and Mr Chamberlain thought that a Minister for Economic Co-ordination would weaken his own position. In both cases there was a definite misunderstanding. What the critics demanded was not better arbitration but more initiative. They did not complain so much that disputes went on too long (though in the case of rearmament there is much evidence that they did), as that in each case the problem needed to be examined by a minister who saw it as a whole and not through the different-coloured spectacles of the several Departments.

The Cabinet is in an even weaker position for this purpose. Twenty-one Departmental ministers have twenty-one sets of problems on their hands. Four or five elder statesmen or junior Cabinet ministers can hardly be expected to bring energy and breadth of vision in a Cabinet whose most important members (apart from the Prime Minister) are engaged in solving hosts of immediate questions arising out of pressing administrative needs.

In this respect the situation has fundamentally altered since Peel presided over his Cabinet of nine "Departmental" and five non-Departmental ministers. The functions of the State controlled by the Cabinet have increased ten-fold or more. The development has been in scope and not merely in depth. The speed of administration has been multiplied since Peel travelled day and night to reach London from Rome in nine days. Leisurely consideration of problems is no longer possible. The difference between Peel and Chamberlain was the difference between a cavalry colonel and the Chief of the Imperial General Staff.

In the sphere of defence, the deficiencies of the Cabinet system were made evident during the Crimean War and the Boer War. The War Office (Reconstitution) Committee pointed out in 1904 that

the British Empire is pre-eminently a great Naval, Indian and Colonial Power. There are, nevertheless, no means for co-ordinating defence problems, for dealing with them as a whole, for defining the proper functions of the various elements, and for ensuring that, on the one hand, peace preparations are carried out upon a consistent plan, and, on the other hand, that, in time of emergency, a definite war policy, based upon solid data, can be formulated.

It was accordingly recommended that the Defence Committee of the Cabinet, set up in 1895, be reconstituted as a Committee of Imperial Defence.

The Committee is not, however, a Cabinet committee. Technically, it advises the Prime Minister, who is its only permanent member, and who summons to each meeting those ministers and officials who are concerned with the items of the agenda. In practice, however, the Treasury, the Foreign Office, the Home Office, the Dominions Office, the Colonial Office, the India Office, the War Office, the Air Ministry, and the Admiralty are always represented. Moreover, the three Chiefs of Staff and the Permanent Secretary to the Treasury may for practical purposes be regarded as permanent members. What is perhaps even more important is that, instead of having a secretary drawn for the occasion from a Department, or an official from the Cabinet Office, it has a permanent secretariat to which officers who have been through the Imperial Staff College are attached. Its concern is not so much with Departmental disputes as with the peace-time formulation of plans for war-time operations. Quite definitely, therefore, its purpose is to think ahead, to plan in the light of all the information available from nine Departments the steps which might have to be taken if war broke out and, with these plans in view, to advise what forces and equipment should be available in the Navy, the Army, and the Air Force. It can take no decisions, but the recommendations of a committee so influential are necessarily received by the Cabinet with very great respect. Moreover, when the Cabinet has decided, the Departments will generally accept the views of the Committee as to what their consequential action should be.

It was inevitably part of the Committee's task to consider the problem of supply. From making recommendations as to the supplies needed to making recommendations for avoiding Departmental competition was but a step. From recommendations relating to armaments to recommendations relating to all supplies required by Departments is only another step. One of its sub-committees, the Supply Board or Principal Supply Officers' Committee, gradually developed a network of committees dealing with the many items which Departments require—oil, motor cars, bicycles, food and the rest. Where necessary, supplies are purchased in bulk. Often one Department buys for the rest. Sometimes it is enough to provide standard contracts, or to enable one Department to use the costing apparatus of another, or to spread buying so that two Departments do not appear on the market at the same time. Nor is this all; joint research in matters like wireless telegraphy, mechanisation, and small arms becomes possible.

The Committee and its warren of sub-committees have thus met many of the problems of co-ordination. It must nevertheless be remembered that its plans had a fairly precise objective. They assumed a war in which Great Britain was engaged. Geography does not change, and scientific invention develops slowly. Leaving "little wars" aside, the number of possible enemies capable of threatening British security at any given time can be counted on the fingers of one hand, and changes in the balance of military and naval power are slow. It is possible to forecast the major enemies and in respect of alliances to assume the worst. On this basis prognostication is not difficult. Forethought and planning are possible because reasonable precision is possible.

It is probable that, given adequate research, social

problems might be tackled in the same way. Trends in population and production can be measured if adequate statistical information is collected. Account can be taken of scientific inventions, though changes may be more rapid and more revolutionary in the economic than in the military field. Wars anywhere in the world necessarily create economic disturbances, and changes in the social structure and economic policies, reacting upon British policy, are more frequent and less easily foreseen. Moreover, war is an occasional event and, when it does arise, the differences of opinion are usually of a technical order. On the other hand, social and economic problems are endemic, and lie at the very centre of political controversy. The task of social and economic planning to meet further conditions is thus more difficult than the task of planning for war; nor can it be hoped that Cabinet decisions can be taken on long-term policies.

In 1925 Mr Baldwin appointed a Committee for Civil Research which was converted into the Economic Research Council by Mr MacDonald in 1930. The Council was modelled on the Committee of Imperial Defence, but the differences in the nature of the problem show that the two bodies could hardly exercise similar functions. If the Council contained experts both inside and outside the civil service, it could give useful advice on the more technical aspects of current policy, but ministers are too intimately concerned with immediate political consequences to hope that occasional committee meetings would be fruitful, and too busy to attend long debates on highly controversial issues. The Council had a permanent secretariat, but it was too small to conduct long-term research, even with the assistance of expert committees. Nor can such a body work successfully if it deals only with questions referred by the Prime Minister. The idea was both too ambitious and not ambitious enough. It was too ambitious because immediate results were expected, and not ambitious enough because not enough scope and money were provided for long-term research. The phrase "Economic General Staff" has often been used, but it is based on a false analogy. The need for more information and more detailed examination of governmental problems is evident, and was pointed out by the Haldane Committee in 1918. A scheme of this kind would not, however, produce immediate results, and its benefits would be indirect. Nobody expects the General Staff to produce a foreign policy, whereas it is apparently thought that an Economic General Staff could solve the problems of unemployment, the cotton industry, the mines, and so on.

This problem in co-ordination is not peculiar to responsible government. It arises in any large-scale undertaking. It seems to have been even greater in pre-war Germany than in pre-war Britain. It is at least as evident in the United States as in this country. Both Germany and the United States had the advantage, however, that the initiative in policy could come from a single individual. Even the restrictions implied in Congressional power (far greater and more serious than those imposed by Parliament) could not prevent Franklin Roosevelt from developing and, in part, carrying out a heroic policy. Much depends, of course, on the personality and the capacity of the President. The policy of the United States had no such forceful direction under Calvin Coolidge. A parallel development in this country could not take place without a further exaltation of the power of the Prime Minister. It has already been suggested that a peace-time Prime Minister ought not to have a policy because the essential source of information is in the Departments. If the Prime Minister were to approach more nearly to the position of an American President, it would be necessary to place the Departmental advisers more closely in relation to Downing Street and so to depress the position of the Departmental ministers. This would be to create a new constitutional system, which might be much better than the present if we could be certain that the Prime Minister was a Roosevelt, but would be very much worse if he were a Harding. What is more likely is that a Prime Minister would develop a second and competing administrative system under his own control. Mr Lloyd George, for instance, had a large secretariat established in temporary buildings in the garden of 10, Downing Street, and therefore known as "the garden suburb". Mr Chamberlain took Sir Horace Wilson out of the Ministry of Labour and made him almost a second Foreign Office. Even Mr Churchill has his own Department, though he has regularised the position by securing his own appointment as Minister of Defence.

If some such system were developed, the problem of co-ordination would not be solved; on the contrary, it would be made more difficult. Instead of providing co-ordination among the Departments, it would create a need for co-ordination between the Prime Minister's office and the Departments as well. There were times after 1918 when the "garden suburb" was following one foreign policy while the Foreign Office was following another; foreign ambassadors secured one answer from the Prime Minister and a different answer from the Foreign Office. The solution of the difficulty must lie in a different direction, by enabling ministers to see their problems from a wide angle, by enabling the Cabinet to grasp the implications of a problem as a whole, and by placing the Prime Minister in such a position that a general oversight of the Departments becomes possible. Such a solution can be secured only by decreasing the number of Departmental ministers and, therefore, of Cabinet ministers.

A reduction in the number of ministers in itself would add to the importance of the discretionary powers of the civil service. It would, therefore, in practice reduce the effective control secured by Parliament through ministerial responsibility. In fact, however, the tendency is in the opposite direction, to increase the number of Departments. The effect of war, it has been pointed out, was to increase the number of Departmental ministers from twenty-one to twenty-seven. Necessarily the consequence is to increase the problem of Departmental co-ordination. It is, however, not necessary that the decrease of the number of Departmental ministers should produce a decrease in the number of ministers. Mr Churchill has shown the way, by placing himself in charge of the Defence Departments, as Minister of Defence, while leaving ordinary administration to the three Departmental ministers. The manner in which the system is working is as yet unknown, though it is unlikely that this island could have been put in a state of defence in six weeks if the ordinary Departmental wrangling (which is always even worse among commissioned officers than it is among civil servants) had continued; also, he has by this device avoided the necessity (felt by Mr Chamberlain) of having the three Departmental ministers in the War Cabinet. There is no reason why this system should not be extended, particularly to the Departments concerned with industry and social services. It was, in fact, recommended by the Haldane Committee in 1918.

The advantages to be obtained are many. At the top there would be a smaller Cabinet, more capable of seeing national problems as a whole and concerned with the political prestige of fewer ministers. The Prime Minister could undertake the essentials of Peel's task by co-ordinating and supplying energy to the work of the Cabinet ministers in matters of primary importance. The

Cabinet ministers themselves would be solely responsible for the co-ordination of the subordinate Departments under their control. Since they would deal only with the major issues of policy, they would be less involved in detailed administration and in a better position to formulate or to secure the formulation of Departmental policy. Disputes between the subordinate Departments would be settled, not by compromise in long committee meetings, but by the decisions of the Cabinet minister. Overlapping and encroachment would be largely avoided by decisions of the Cabinet minister which would be binding on the subordinate Departments. There would be no divergent policies among the subordinate Departments, since major policy which did not go to the Cabinet would be settled by the Cabinet minister, and Departmental policy could operate only within the limits prescribed by his policy. Ministerial responsibility would be increased, because more ministers would be present in the House of Commons. There would be minor changes in the technique of asking and answering questions, but they would involve no more difficult problems than the present relation between questions answered by Departmental ministers and questions answered by the Prime Minister. Indeed, there would be none of the confusion which sometimes results where—as with the treatment of aliens recently—ministers can disclaim responsibility because the Departmental functions overlap and each Department can blame the other.

CHAPTER VIII

GOVERNMENT IN
WAR TIME

§ 1. *Parliament*

No British Government would dare to declare war against a great power without the almost unanimous support of the people. Totalitarian war cannot be waged on party lines. It is true that "punitive expeditions" can be sent against rebellious tribesmen in spite of the criticisms of the Opposition. It is true also that the Boer War was begun when the Liberal party believed that it could have been avoided. Modern wars are not of that kind. A democracy must have the same unity as a totalitarian State. The difference lies in the methods of achieving unity. In a country where opponents are as free as supporters to express their opinions, it must be reached by free persuasion. A subject people must be coerced; a free people must be convinced. This is indeed one of the reasons for believing that the future of the world—if it has a future—lies in democracy; for there is nothing that the citizen hates more than modern warfare, and his convictions must be strong if his repugnance is to be overcome. Democracies may be slow and blind; they cannot be aggressors.

These assertions were true of 1939, but they were not so true of 1914. Even in 1914, however, the Liberal Government could not have declared war if it had not been convinced, after the German invasion of Belgium, that public opinion was persuaded that war was necessary. In 1939 the conviction was stronger. The Chamberlain Government had tried honestly to appease the appetite of the dictators. The Opposition parties had pointed out the dangers and had vehemently opposed both men and measures. When, in March 1939, the Government had been convinced of its failure, British foreign policy was virtually on an all-party basis (except in relation to Russia). No Government formed out of the then House of Commons, and no Government which could successfully have appealed to the people, could have acted otherwise in the six months from March to September. In 1939 as in 1914 the nation was virtually unanimous.

In such conditions the nature of the parliamentary contest must necessarily be changed. In 1914 the Conservative Opposition offered its support for a policy of war even before the Liberal Government had made up its mind. Political relations were then far more acrimonious than they have been at any time since, because Home Rule, the House of Lords and the Welsh Church were matters of acute controversy. In spite of some difficulties, the matters under debate were suspended, and the Conservative Opposition gave support to the Government until, in May 1915, disputes in the Admiralty induced the leaders to intimate privately that they could no longer give support. A Coalition Government was at once formed, and thenceforward there was no Opposition until after the general election of 1918.

In August 1939, the House of Commons gave emergency powers to the National Government by a majority of 427 to 4, and on 2 September voted for conscription by 340 to 7. Mr Chamberlain at once offered representation in the War Cabinet to the Labour party and representation in the Government to the Liberal party.

Neither accepted, but henceforth there was no real opposition until May 1940. As in 1914, an electoral truce was arranged, whereby the three major parties agreed not to oppose each others' candidates at by-elections. The Deputy Leader of the Opposition described his attitude on 13 September as that of a "candid friend", and stated that the function of the Opposition was two-fold, to express the opinion of the people on the statements, the legislation and the proposals of the Government, and to bring the troubles of the people before the Government. Opposition speakers at a later stage objected to the use of the phrase "party truce". In fact, however, the Government refrained from making controversial proposals, and consulted the Opposition leaders on matters of policy. The Opposition obstructed no legislation, accepted financial proposals, and refrained from embarrassing the conduct of the war by inconvenient debates. Proposals not strictly cognate to the war, such as part of the Old Age and Widows' Pensions Bill, were opposed with all the fervour of peace time. Special problems, such as those of food supply, man-power, shipping, propaganda, and the rest, were debated and even voted upon. Minor details of Government proposals, such as the additional sugar tax, the railway agreement, the unemployment insurance regulations, and the rest, were debated and even opposed. Between the outbreak of war and 8 May 1940, the Opposition challenged sixty-eight divisions.

The position of "candid friend" is, however, difficult to maintain. In 1914 and 1915 the Conservatives became more and more candid and less and less friendly. In the end they realised that they must either oppose or share the responsibility. In the early months of the present war, Labour members found themselves in the same position. They had approved of the declaration of war, and they wished to do nothing to hinder its successful

prosecution.   Nevertheless, there was growing dissatisfaction over the slowness of supply, the failure to
utilise man-power and wealth, and the dilatoriness and
weakness of economic organisation. The collapse of
Finland was followed by a "timid" Budget, and the
Budget by the withdrawal from Southern Norway.

The solution of May 1915 was not open. Labour
leaders were not prepared to join the "Munich triumvirate"—Mr Chamberlain, Sir John Simon and Sir
Samuel Hoare. When the withdrawal from Southern
Norway threw them into Opposition, it was necessary
to have not merely a Coalition Government but a new
Prime Minister. The withdrawal was, however, the
occasion and not the cause. There cannot be opposition
in war time, and candid friends can sit on the back
benches but not on the Front Opposition Bench. War
demands a coalition, as Mr Chamberlain realised in
September 1939. What Mr Chamberlain did not realise,
was that if there could be no coalition under him there
had to be a coalition under somebody else. The fall of
the Chamberlain Government was not due to the fact
that forty-one of his supporters voted against him—
though that fact underlined the proposition—but to
the fact that the Opposition had decided to oppose.
Mr Chamberlain's appeal to his "friends" was the gravest
misunderstanding of a parliamentary situation since his
father retired from active politics. A Prime Minister in
war time ought to have no parliamentary "friends"
because he ought to have no parliamentary enemies. If
he has to fight in the House as well as in the field, he must
make way for a Prime Minister who can concentrate his
forces against his country's enemies.

The spirit of parliamentary proceedings is fundamentally altered when a comprehensive Government like
Mr Churchill's Coalition is in office. The procedure of
the House assumes, in fact if not in form, that opinion is

divided along party lines. With a coalition there can be no such party divisions. Moreover, in war time the Government demands and receives powers wide enough to take the necessary action without parliamentary approval. The Emergency Powers (Defence) Acts, 1939 and 1940, have given immense powers for government by Order in Council.

It must not be assumed, however, that temporarily there is a dictatorship. Parliament continues to meet for three days a week during longer sessions than are customary in time of peace. Ministers are still compelled to answer questions, to listen to debates, and to answer criticisms. Indeed, legislation must still be introduced because, wide though the emergency powers are, they are far from absolute. It is unnecessary for us to consider in detail the provisions of the emergency legislation; but, for instance, it contains no power to tax (subject to very minor qualifications) without express parliamentary approval. The produce of taxation cannot be used for war purposes or otherwise without legislation. Any increase in the present limited powers of borrowing requires an Act of Parliament. No changes in the social services or other peace-time services can be made without new legislation. No action can be taken (for instance, to guarantee to allotment holders that they will not be turned out immediately at the end of the war) except in Parliament if action may be required at the end of the war. Only minor changes can be made in the administration of civil and criminal justice under powers conferred by the emergency legislation. In other words, what the Government has are sufficient powers (other than financial) for waging war. Everything else, including the financing of the war, remains definitely under parliamentary control.

These legal limitations are important, because they show that parliamentary action remains as necessary in war as in peace. In fact, Parliament passed more legislation between 24 August 1939, when it granted the emergency powers, and the end of August 1940 than it normally passes in two years. Even after the initial spate of emergency measures had ceased, in the session which began at the end of November 1939 it has passed as much legislation as in a normal session. Far more important than the legal situation, however, is the spirit in which government is carried on. To enact legislation is no more than one-half of Parliament's function. Its main task is to stimulate and to criticise. It was in the House of Commons that Mr Chamberlain was convinced that the country required a change of Government. Though there can be no formal opposition to a Government supported by 99 per cent of the members of the House, the odd 1 per cent is permitted to express without limitation its opposition to the war itself. Private members on both "sides" of the House (though the House now has one side only) continue to stimulate and to criticise. Where some action is disapproved, members do not hesitate to say so, and even to vote against the Government. On one occasion recently (a debate on civil liberties, be it noted) the Government's majority fell to twenty-eight. Indeed, nothing shows more emphatically the essentially democratic nature of our war-time government than the debates on the internment of aliens, the exercise of powers of arrest without trial, and the creation of special criminal courts. These debates occurred, too, in July and August 1940, when German guns could fire across the English Channel, when from a ring of bases from the Arctic to the Bay of Biscay invasion of these islands was being threatened, when German fighters and bombers were seeking supremacy in British air, and when two-thirds of the broadcasting stations in Europe were prophesying the immediate downfall of the British Empire. While these conditions were in operation,

Parliament was insisting (and was compelling the Government to give way) that innocent aliens ought not to be interned, that popular opinion ought not to be suppressed, and that trial by courts martial was not justified even in war time. In truth, there was the same deference to parliamentary opinion, the same recognition of fundamental liberties, the same process of persuasion, as in time of peace. It was not only magnificent, it was democratic war. Indeed, the criticism to be advanced is not that Parliament was reduced to an impotent subservience, but that, on the contrary, in its liking for secret sessions it was tending to seize arbitrary and unconstitutional power—though fortunately there was evidence that public opinion was making its weight felt. This is indeed a total war not because, on both sides of the narrow seas, whole nations are regimented for war under dictatorial control, but because, on this side, the whole nation is engaged in it, in Downing Street, in Westminster and, what is more, in Lambeth Walk.

§ 2. *War Administration*

The ordinary mechanism of government is necessarily slow. At every stage it requires the resolution of conflicts of opinion and (what are often the same) conflicts of interest. A dictatorship does not necessarily act more speedily than a democracy. An over-developed bureaucracy like that of Germany is often clumsier than a simple hierarchy like that of Great Britain. In this respect Germany has three advantages only. In the first place, the power of decision is often vested in a single person, whereas with us it is more often vested in a committee. When an issue has come up from the bureaucracy to the Führer, for instance, he alone takes it, whereas with us it is taken by the Cabinet. This system produces quicker results, however, only where the issue reaches the Führer more quickly than it reaches the Cabinet; and in peace time, at least, the advantage seems to have been on the British side. On the other hand, if the question for determination does not come from the hierarchy but is, so to speak, injected directly at the top, the Germans might have the advantage. A dictator accustomed to think hard and quickly does not need to have his decision put down on a committee agenda for discussion at the first available opportunity. Whether Hitler has this capacity is by no means proved —such evidence as there is is contradictory. Communing with the stars in the eyrie at Berchtesgaden may take as long as communing with colleagues at 10 Downing Street. It is nevertheless clear that, with ordinary men, the machine ought in this respect to be more efficient.

In the second place, the leadership principle ought to produce quicker execution. The Cabinet orders, like Hitler; but a democratic system assumes a right to criticise even past decisions. A dictatorship is like an army where orders must be obeyed and not discussed. If the Light Brigade is ordered to charge, charge it must. The Leader's commands, and the commands of all inferior leaders, must similarly be obeyed until they are countermanded.

In the third place—though this is really an instance of the second advantage—a dictator has no Parliament. He has the legal powers already, and he does not need to persuade a "set of fellows" that he ought to have them. Hitler has not to be in his place in the Reichstag to answer questions or to reply to criticisms.

It must not be assumed that these advantages are very great. It is probably true to say that in peace time the British system was more efficient than the German. Appearances to the contrary were due largely to the fact that the initiative inevitably lies with the aggressor. The burglar always has the advantage over the police, because he matures his plans at leisure. He is more often caught after the act than in the act. In the first few months of war the situation is inevitably the same. Nevertheless, the leisure of the aggressor makes even more necessary the speed of the resistance. Wars cannot be won by the methods of peace. Movement must be followed by counter movement, attack by counter attack.

Armed forces are necessarily organised on the leadership principle. Their policy is, however, determined by the civilian control. War, said a famous French statesman, is too serious a matter to be left to generals and admirals. It is urgently necessary that this control should be speedy and effective. Moreover, the whole apparatus of production and supply is in civilian hands and under civilian control. Civil defence, too, is a matter of civilian organisation.

One element of delay can be removed by taking special powers such as those conferred by the Emergency Powers (Defence) Acts, 1939 and 1940, and by the later Defence of the Realm Acts in the war of 1914–18. The various "controls" of the Ministries of Supply and Food have never received the express approval of Parliament because they have been set up under Regulation 55 of the Defence Regulations, which can be amended and expanded merely by Order in Council. It is true that Parliament can always debate these matters. Certain provisions of the Defence Regulations relating to civil liberties were amended after debate in the House. Nevertheless, the powers can be taken without the delay involved in parliamentary debate and a compromise between urgency and democracy is obtained by allowing Parliament to criticise after action has been taken. Even this method impedes administration somewhat, because Ministers are required to be in their places to answer questions and reply to criticisms. The House of Commons exercises a wise restraint by allowing much of the parliamentary process to be left in the hands of Parliamentary Secretaries.

It is never true, however, that the greatest delay occurs in Parliament. The process of administration is inevitably longer and more complicated in a vast bureaucracy than in a simple hierarchy of the British type. In the lower ranks of administration speed and efficiency depend essentially on the qualities of the civil service. The great difficulty in war time is that the civil service has to be rapidly expanded to undertake new functions. In so far as this process involves the more rapid promotion of able young civil servants who would in peace time occupy less responsible positions until vacancies were available, it is wholly beneficial. The war of 1914–18 accelerated the promotion of people like Sir Warren Fisher, Sir John Anderson, Sir William Beveridge and Sir Arthur Salter. There is, however, the danger that such promotions, both to the highest posts and to posts of responsibility in the lower ranks of the administrative class, will place burdens on officials who are not competent to bear them. Civil servants necessarily doubt the capacity of persons, however eminent in their own fields, brought in from outside. They tend to recommend the appointment of less competent civil servants rather than more able outsiders whose administrative competence has yet to be proved. Moreover, there is always the professional fear that persons who gain lucrative posts in an emergency will hold them when the war comes to an end. During the present war, for instance, there has been a general tendency to give to outsiders salaries less than they were earning in civil life, in the hope that, at the end of the war, they would return to their more lucrative civil employment: but since salary and responsibility in the civil service are roughly commensurate, the result is that the highest intelligence is being wasted in routine work.

There is, too, the difficulty that the normal methods of recruitment cannot be employed for the enlistment of temporary civil servants. The carefully devised precautions against favouritism have to be swept away. It says much for the civil-service tradition that no allegations have been made of political "jobs". The allegations have related not to favouritism by ministers or influence by members of Parliament but to favouritism by civil servants. Friends and even relatives of senior civil servants have figured somewhat prominently in parliamentary questions. No one can visit any of the mushroom Departments or glance at a list of temporary employees without feeling that social prestige as well as ability have been taken into consideration. Everyone knows of persons employed because they were recommended by or to a senior civil servant. This difficulty, which was prominent in 1914–18, was recognised before the present war, and an attempt was made to meet it by establishing the National Central Register of persons with special qualifications. In the present war, however, the initial appointments were the most important and recommendations and not qualifications filed in the National Central Register was for these the basis of appointment. The Register has been fully used for subsequently created posts, but in the meantime mischief might have been done.

How important these difficulties are cannot be estimated. It is certainly unwise to take at their face value statements made in Parliament. Much of the criticism of the Ministry of Information in the early months of the war was clearly misinformed. Some of the criticisms of the Ministry of Economic Warfare clearly came from civil-service organisations anxious to protect their members against competition from talented outsiders, and were evidence of the very danger that has to be avoided. On the whole it may be presumed that orthodoxy has been a greater danger than unorthodoxy. It cannot be alleged that senior posts have been filled by "socialite" nincompoops; it can be alleged, however, that administrative ability outside the civil service has not been fully utilised, or used in the best way.

Indeed, orthodox methods of administration may be too dilatory for war time. Ministerial responsibility has for its consequence the rule that civil servants must not make mistakes. Decisions are taken slowly and after the most careful consideration. In war time any rapid decision which is not obviously foolish is better than a delayed decision which, if taken in time, would have been perfect. A good war-time administrator deliberately runs the risk of making mistakes. The commander of the Allied forces in Flanders in May 1940 had to decide between two dangerous alternatives, to break through the German corridor or embark such troops as he could on the coast. The historians of the war may be able to decide which was the better alternative. What the commander could not do was to dither for a week or a month while his staff wrote memoranda, attended committees, consulted experts, and the rest. Any immediate decision was better than a delayed decision. The task of a civil administrator is not essentially different. What is wanted, as Mr Herbert Morrison said when he was in Opposition, is "drive, determination and decision".

Whether these qualities are possessed by the senior civil servants cannot be answered by an outside observer. It has at least been possible for a responsible journal to assert:

For twenty years since the last war, two insidious tendencies have been at work: on the one hand, a concentration of authority in the hands of a very small group of senior officials; on the other, the deliberate inculcation among these senior officials of a spirit of small-minded timidity. Almost any argument will be accepted in the higher ranks of the civil service for *not* doing anything. As a result of this spirit and the bottle-necks created by the concentration of authority and by the dominance of the Treasury (which has been allowed to extend over policy as well as over expenditure, over the appointment of persons to do tasks as well as over the creation of the positions they hold), the sluggishness of Government Departments has become a national danger. Decisions that should require days take months, and then they are half-hearted.[1]

This assertion may be exaggerated or even false. It represents, however, the kind of impression which could prevail while Mr Chamberlain was Prime Minister. If it contains any element of truth, the responsibility must be with the ministers who have controlled Departments, and especially with Prime Ministers. It is the business of ministers to see that they receive rapid and precise recommendations. If they do not, they must change the personnel concerned where they have the power, or insist that the Prime Minister make the change where the appointment rests (as it does in the case of the most senior officials) with him. A statement of this kind is an accusation against ministers as well as against civil servants. In war time ministers must be as ruthless with their advisers as M. Reynaud was with his generals in May 1940.

Parliament has realised that energy must be injected into the governmental machine at the top. This explains the growing criticism which led to the resignation of Mr Chamberlain in May 1940. It explains also the principle on which Mr Churchill made most of his appointments in the new Government. In fact, the method adopted where greater energy was needed was the creation of new Departments under ministerial control, for instance, those of Supply, Shipping, Aircraft Production and Petroleum. It is, however, evident that

[1] *The Economist*, 25 May 1940, p. 925.

the creation of new Departments increases the problem of co-ordination.

Much has been said on this subject in Chapter VII. In time of war it is all the more urgent, and it does not follow that peace-time methods are the most effective. Nevertheless, Mr Chamberlain used peace-time methods. Indeed, by reducing the number of Departmental ministers in the Cabinet he made peace-time methods more difficult just when the problem became more acute. His War Cabinet could deal with matters affecting Foreign Affairs, the Treasury and the armed forces, but the other Departments were no longer represented. Instead, he developed the peace-time committee system. There was, for instance, an Economic Co-ordination Committee under the Chancellor of the Exchequer, with an inter-departmental committee of officials below it; a Ministerial Priority Committee under the Minister for the Co-ordination of Defence, with five priority sub-committees presided over by parliamentary secretaries; a Civil Defence Committee under the Minister of Home Security; a Home Policy Committee under the Lord Privy Seal; an Economic Warfare Committee under the Minister of Economic Policy, together with an inter-departmental committee of officials under the Director-General of the Ministry; and an Export Policy Committee under the Minister of Food.

The committee system is admirable for ordinary administration. It provides that every question be fully considered from every angle. It enables the accumulated wisdom and experience of the Departments to be brought to bear on every problem. It permits conflicts of opinion to be resolved by persuasion or compromise. It ensures that party government be carried on by a Ministry working as a team in spite of differences of approach. It is, however, extremely slow and time-wasting. What is wanted in war time is not the best decision that can be reached by discussion and compromise, but the best decision that can be reached quickly. A minister of sound judgment who can take rapid decisions is infinitely to be preferred to the best committee in our committee-ridden country. There is no time for debate; the minister who is not prepared to be ruthlessly overruled ought not to be a war-time minister; compromises lead to defeat.

Nothing demonstrates more clearly the weakness of the Chamberlain Government than the example which Mr Chamberlain gave, as typical of the whole range of functions, in the debate on economic co-ordination on 1 February 1940. It related to the supply of raw materials; but it is impossible to give a summary because his explanation of the process occupied 128 lines in the *Official Report*. It is probably simpler than it sounds, and it really is not typical because priority of supplies is a problem affecting all Departments and not a few only. Nevertheless, Mr Chamberlain gave this explanation to show the simplicity of the whole procedure and to prove that no changes were necessary.

It may be stated as a general proposition that, wherever possible, a committee should be superseded by a minister. Mr Churchill has recognised it by taking upon himself the functions of a Minister of Defence. It is true that he has also appointed a Defence Committee, consisting of three Departmental ministers and their Chiefs of Staff. There is, however, a great difference between Mr Churchill's and Mr Chamberlain's War Committee. As Chairman of the Chamberlain Defence Committee, Mr Churchill had to persuade the Committee to reach a decision by discussion and, if necessary, compromise. As Minister of Defence in his own Government, Mr Churchill is "assisted" by the Committee. That is, he hears what they have to say and then gives them orders. It is the difference between a British

Cabinet and an American Cabinet; it is almost the difference between a commander's council of war and the Council of the League of Nations. Moreover, Mr Churchill is not limited to the advice which he receives in the Committee. Presumably he can summon any staff officer to express a personal opinion. In any case, he has his own staff under General Ismay, the former Secretary to the Committee of Imperial Defence.

The Prime Minister did not extend this system to other departments of activity. There was a Production Council under Mr Greenwood, an Economic Policy Committee under Mr Greenwood, a Food Policy Committee under Mr Attlee, a Home Policy Committee under Mr Attlee, and a Civil Defence Committee under Sir John Anderson. These five committees were co-ordinated by another committee under Mr Chamberlain. This system seems to show a failure to appreciate the lessons which Mr Churchill had learned in the sphere of defence. In war time committees are useful to give advice, but the chairman, and not the committee, should decide. In other words, what is wanted is not merely a super-Minister of Defence but also super-Ministers of Production, Economic Policy and Home Policy. Normal Departmental decisions can then be taken by the Departments; but each super-minister, with the aid of a committee and a separate staff, can take decisions of major importance which do not go to the War Cabinet.

It has been urged that such a system destroys ministerial responsibility. It has already been pointed out that such an argument illustrates how slogans become arguments without having reason behind them. Ministerial responsibility does not mean that there must be twenty-seven ministers, each solely responsible for the work of his Department. Nor does it mean that co-operation among ministers must be secured only by agreement. A Cabinet, or a committee authorised by a

Cabinet, can always overrule or give orders to a minister, whether he is a member of the Cabinet or committee or not. Nor does ministerial responsibility mean that one minister cannot act under the control of another. The President of the Board of Trade has three ministers subject to his control—the Parliamentary Secretaries to the Overseas Trade Department, to the Mines Department, and to the Petroleum Department. Ministerial responsibility means only that some minister must be responsible to Parliament for every administrative act. The addition of a super-minister to the official hierarchy, in place of a committee, does not destroy ministerial responsibility; it increases it, because it adds another responsible minister.

This argument was not used by Mr Chamberlain in the debate on economic co-ordination on 1 February 1940, but he used about ten other arguments. Some of these depended on a complete misunderstanding. Mr Herbert Morrison had asked for an Economic Minister capable of direction, decision and drive. He was not to have merely a power of reconciliation or co-ordination: but Mr Chamberlain thought that what was asked for was an "arbiter". In this he followed Mr Baldwin's example: when demands were made for a minister to direct re-armament, Mr Baldwin appointed a lawyer to decide disputes between the defence departments. As has been explained in the preceding chapter, co-ordination involves much more than settling disputes.

Mr Chamberlain also said that the addition of a super-minister would "over-elaborate the hierarchy"; in fact, however, it would replace an elaborate committee machinery by a minister with a few advisers. He asserted that the super-minister might be wrong and the Departmental minister right. So they might: but so might a committee or a Cabinet. It is quite certain that if the present system involves delay, nobody will be right.

Mr Chamberlain doubted whether there were any super-men to hold this kind of office. The unkind critic might remark that they were certainly not in his War Cabinet; but in fact the request was not for a superman but for a man instead of a committee. Finally, he said that such a minister would "challenge the position of the Prime Minister". It is perhaps enough to say that when the failure of the Norwegian expedition created parlia-mentary difficulties Mr Chamberlain found it possible to convert Mr Churchill into something approaching a Minister of Defence. The real answer is, however, that the Prime Minister's authority would be increased, be-cause he would need only to co-ordinate a handful of ministers instead of twenty-seven and could therefore do it more effectively. These and less important arguments put by Mr Chamberlain are easily answered by pointing out, above all, that individuals of any capacity neces-sarily act more speedily than committees, and speed is the essential requisite.

§ 3. *War Cabinets*

That the peace-time Cabinet system is not speedy enough for war government was the consideration which induced Lloyd George and Bonar Law to overthrow the Asquith Coalition in 1916. Until the end of that year, decisions had been taken by the whole Cabinet after discussion in a large War Council. The result was long committee meetings, followed by long Cabinet meetings, and appalling delay. When Mr Lloyd George became Prime Minister, he suppressed the ordinary Cabinet, and replaced it by a War Cabinet whose membership was never less than five and never more than seven. None of its members, except the Chancellor of the Exchequer, had Departmental duties.

This system made for more rapid decisions, but it had

three defects. First, the Cabinet ministers often had no prior knowledge of the problem brought before them and must, therefore, have taken valuable time in reading documents and generally in informing themselves about the background of each question. Secondly, and as a consequence, Departmental ministers with their advisers had to attend meetings of the War Cabinet at which questions affecting their Departments were under discussion. They had thus to waste time in making a case and, where two Departments were concerned, in debating the issue. Thirdly, since the War Cabinet could deal only with major issues ripe for determination, its members had to spend much time as chairmen of Cabinet committees at which co-ordination was attempted.

Perhaps it was knowledge of these defects which induced Mr Chamberlain to try another plan at the outbreak of the present war. His War Cabinet contained nine members (afterwards reduced to eight). Of these, five were Departmental ministers—the Chancellor of the Exchequer, the Foreign Secretary, and the heads of the three Defence Departments. In addition, the Minister for the Co-ordination of Defence was a member until April 1940. The idea was, no doubt, to include in the War Cabinet those ministers who were more directly concerned with the war. If so, there was complete miscalculation as to the nature of the war, since totalitarian war requires the use of all weapons, and the postponement of the *Blitzkrieg* made economic warfare, food production, labour, shipping and supply the essential problems during the first eight months. In any case, the balance was false, since it under-emphasised the importance of the Home Front. Moreover, ministers controlling large Departments like the Admiralty, the War Office and the Air Ministry cannot afford the time to attend daily Cabinet meetings, and have no energy to spare for aspects of the war outside their Departments. Finally, the War Cabinet was too big. The smaller the Committee, the more speedily and the more effectively it can reach decisions.

Mr Churchill at first returned to Mr Lloyd George's example. He made, however, one significant modification by taking to himself the office of Minister of Defence. If he can bear the double burden, this is an admirable solution of that side of the problem. As Minister of Defence he should be familiar with all those problems of the three Defence Departments which are of sufficient importance to require a Cabinet decision. In the first place the three Departments are co-ordinated not by a Committee but by a single minister. In the second place the Departmental minister can decide day-to-day details without the constant interruption of Cabinet meetings. In the third place the essential problems of the three Services are known to the Prime Minister and can therefore be explained without summoning ministers and Chiefs of Staff—though their presence may be required when major issues have to be settled. The solution is so admirable that it ought to be extended by giving the other Cabinet ministers, other than the Foreign Secretary, the same kind of control over groups of Departments or groups of functions. Mr Greenwood would be far more effective, for instance, if he were not merely Chairman of the Production Council, but Minister for Production, working with and through the Ministers of Supply and Labour. The case for super-ministers has already been put as a means of co-ordination—it is also a case for a more effective War Cabinet.

CHAPTER IX

BRITISH DEMOCRACY

§ 1. *Government and Opinion*

The fact which emerges most clearly from the survey in this book is the close relation between the policies followed by the Government and the general ideas of the majority of the electorate. It is a consequence of the simple principles upon which the British Constitution is based. The Government governs because it has a majority in the House of Commons. It possesses that majority because the party which it leads secured a majority of seats at the last general election. The parties are not mere electioneering organisations, as they tend to be in Canada and the United States, but are truly based upon competing political principles. In preferring one party to another, therefore, the electorate not only prefers one Government to another but prefers one line of policy to another. Its choice is of course made at infrequent intervals, but always the Government in power has the prospect of having to appeal to the electorate at no very distant date. If it wishes to remain in power it must continue to receive the support of a majority. It must be able to base a successful appeal on its past record. It must be able to explain away its mistakes and emphasise its achievements. Every mistake is an argument against it and every achievement an argument for it. Therefore it must not make obvious mistakes, and its achievements must be such as will meet the electors' approval. Since in fact the division of support between the two major parties is extremely small, any Government must have profound respect for movements of opinion. Nor can it fail to be aware of such movements, for every member of the House of Commons is in close touch with his constituency and is aware of the currents that tend to lose him votes. He will lose votes from every unpopular action by his leaders because he is elected not on his personality nor on his political record but on his party label. A vote against the Government is a vote against him. Accordingly, he expresses in the House or in the lobbies the fear that the Government policy induces in him. He sounds the alarm in the House when the bell begins to ring in his constituency.

The history of the Chamberlain Government convinces many that this analysis is not correct. They are so convinced because they—and particularly Americans—find it incredible that the majority of the electorate supported Mr Chamberlain. The opponents of a Government always find it incredible that its supporters are such fools, and many British subjects found American isolationism equally incredible. There is no evidence that, at any time before May 1940, Mr Chamberlain had lost his majority. In 1935 Mr Baldwin had secured 432 seats out of 615. Munich was supported by 366 votes to 144, no member of a Government party voting with the Opposition. These figures are not representative of opinion in the country. Allowing for unopposed returns, it may be estimated that the Baldwin Government gained about 54·5 per cent of the votes in 1935. There is no precise method of weighing changes of opinion between general elections. In particular, bye-election results are of no value unless the changes are very pronounced. A close analysis suggests, however, that the Government lost support slightly between the resignation of Mr Eden in February 1938 and the Munich agreement of September of that year. The loss was no greater after Munich, and it seems to have been recovered after the invasion of Czechoslovakia in March 1939. All the portents suggest that if there had been no war in 1939 and a general election had taken place the Government would have obtained a majority, though probably more nearly proportionate to its majority in the country. Mr Chamberlain had not lost his majority in the House even in May 1940, and there is no evidence that he had lost it in the country. As has been said, what compelled him to resign was not the fact that forty-one of his former supporters voted against him (though that drove home the lesson) but the fact that the Labour party had decided to oppose. In war time opposition must be avoided, and since "the Munich triumvirate" was the cause of the opposition, it was clear that resignation was necessary.

Some qualifications must nevertheless be made to the general statement made above. In the first place it must be made clear that the electorate and the people are not quite the same body. True it is that all adults have the vote, but some of them have two votes. The business premises qualification and, to a less degree, the university qualification, give certain classes of the population, notably the professional classes and small traders, an advantage which accrues, generally, to the Conservative party. The number of such votes is somewhere in the region of six millions; but it is probable that many of these "double votes" are not cast. A few of the people concerned—mostly university graduates—have three or four votes and, though the number of these extra votes is counted among the "electorate", they cannot legally be cast.

It would be absurd to insist on the principle of "one man (or woman), one vote" as essential to democracy.

According to this test, many of the American States, including all the Southern States, would not be democratic. Nor would France have passed the test. Indeed, it is still possible to argue that the middle classes ought to have more weight than the working classes, not because their interest ought to be specially protected but because, it is alleged, they have a better understanding of the intricacy of the problems of government. The truth of the allegation is, to say the least, extremely doubtful. Moreover, the argument assumes that the middle classes use political power not in their own interest but in the interest of the people at large—a proposition which all history demonstrates to be false. There is strength in the argument that an illiterate electorate is likely to be led astray by unscrupulous demagogues; but, in the first place, the British people is not illiterate and, in the second place, reason and experience show that the necessary educational facilities are made available very slowly, if at all, so long as they are deprived of the vote.

Secondly, the power of public opinion can operate only where there is a powerful party system which gives the electors a real alternative. In Great Britain this condition is satisfied, though the existence of the double vote places certain constituencies in the pocket of the Conservative party. In Northern Ireland, however, it is not satisfied. Seven of the thirteen seats were not contested in 1935, and the other six were contested only by republicans—successfully in Fermanagh and Tyrone. No change of opinion can affect the ten seats which the Unionist party holds in Ulster. The answer to this objection is, no doubt, that if Ulster opinion changed there would be other candidates. Civil liberties are not so well protected in Northern Ireland as they are in Great Britain, but there is nothing to prevent the Labour party from conducting propaganda there.

Thirdly, the constituencies are no longer in accord with the distribution of population. Even in 1918 the element of size as well as of population was brought in, thus giving an advantage to the rural voter. Recent population changes have given an advantage to the industrial worker at the expense of the middle-class vote in the suburbs and the suburbanised country districts. In the party sense, these modifications of the principle of electoral equality probably cancel each other. Moreover, a mathematical equality is never possible, and it is probable that the homogeneity of the British population provides for a more nearly equal representative principle in the United Kingdom than in most other democracies.

Fourthly, our system of representation produces the result that the size of a majority in the House of Commons may bear little relationship to the size of the majority in the country. In 1935, for instance, the Conservative party and its dependents gained, allowing for uncontested seats, about 54·5 per cent of the votes but 70 per cent of the seats. The consequences have been discussed in Chapter II, where it is suggested that the advantages of proportional representation are not so great as the disadvantages. In any case, proportional representation usually means not government by the people but government by groups. The argument on which this part of the chapter is based is that because the Government has a majority and because it wishes to retain that majority it is and must be extremely susceptible to changes of opinion in the constituencies. In all probability a coalition based on groups would be far less susceptible, because movements of opinion would be obscured and political crises would depend very largely on personal sympathies and antipathies. It is important that every section of opinion should have its instrument of expression, but not that it should be proportionately represented in the House.

This brings us to the fifth point, that the opinions which weigh most heavily are not the large sections but what may be called the "marginal" opinion, represented by the floating vote. The nature and size of that vote have already been discussed. The result in the pre-war political situation was to emphasise the lower middle-class opinion in the suburbs and suburbanised county districts —just that section of opinion which is in fact under-represented through shifts in the population and the development of large-scale production. It is of course true that no party dares to antagonise the main body of its supporters, but at present neither can gain a majority without capturing the marginal votes. No representative system can avoid this result. Proportional representation, in fact, would exaggerate it by placing the balance of the Constitution in the hands of an organised group at least as capable of using it for the personal advantage of its leaders as for the benefit of the marginal voters. Nor has any other system avoided the result. Even in presidential elections in the United States the "key" States are known, and the electoral college system has enormously exaggerated it. Moreover, combined with the irresponsibility of the executive, the strength of minorities has led to the practice of the organised lobby and the pork-barrel.

The sixth point arises out of the fifth. This middle-class margin is politically timid. It has a precarious foothold on the middle rungs of the social ladder. It fears to drop lower and hopes tenaciously to climb a little higher. It is, therefore, very susceptible to rumour and panic. It has what may be called a *Daily Mail* and *Daily Express* type of mind; these newspapers in fact cater primarily for this type of reader, as their advertisement columns bear witness. Stories about "red-letters" and the use of savings are readily accepted, and a depression like that of 1931 sends it running for shelter.

It is thus a convenient soil for the cynical empiricism of the Conservative Central Office which the almost equal cynicism of Transport House cannot offset.

This is, however, one application of a general problem, that public opinion is apt to be swayed not by reason and knowledge but by emotion and propaganda. The parties are in fact vast propaganda machines. On the one hand the Conservative party beats the mystical drum of patriotism and on the other hand the Labour party plays the shrill fife of social sympathy—"allows its bleeding heart to go to its bloody head". This is a characteristic of all democracies. It is, however, still more a characteristic of dictatorships, as every reader of *Mein Kampf*, every spectator of fascist or Nazi circuses, and every listener to German and Italian broadcasts, can testify. The difference is that in a democracy the elector can choose between the drum and the fife, whereas in the dictatorships he has to choose between the drum (or the trombone) and the rubber truncheon. The result in Great Britain is that the ordinary elector has a good deal of suspicion of all the instruments of the political orchestra. He is apt to "confound their politics" (in more Anglo-Saxon language) and turn to the racing results. He retains enough interest to vote, but votes according to what he believes to be his interest. In consequence he is accused by the Marxists of not being "politically conscious". It is true that he is not conscious of the Marxist interpretation of history and hates class war as much as he hates imperialist war; but he is fully conscious either of the importance of unionism, in which case he votes Labour, or of the importance of financial stability, in which case he votes Conservative. There are, of course, cross-currents, especially among the middle classes. Roman Catholics generally believe that there is some connection between socialism and atheism; the Church of England generally induces a mild

Conservatism; the Free Churches are apt to be radical, especially in Wales and Scotland; and the League of Nations Union and other intellectual movements help to sway the marginal votes. John Stuart Mill's rationalist assumptions are largely false, but the British voter has a sound and steady empiricism which he calls "common sense".

It is sometimes said that the Government in power is able to delude the people by neglecting to give unpalatable information and making comfortable forecasts which it knows to be false. Emphasis is naturally laid on the speech of Mr Baldwin on 12 November 1936, in which, with "appalling frankness", he confessed that at the election of 1935 he had asked for a mandate for "the establishment of a settled peace" through the use of the League of Nations machinery when he knew that the nature of German preparations required a mandate for rearmament. He justified his action by pointing to the general "pacifist" opinion in the country, as exhibited particularly at the Fulham bye-election of 1933, and by asserting that the country would not have accepted any other policy:

Supposing I had gone to the country and said that Germany was rearming and that we must rearm, does anybody think that this pacific democracy would have rallied to that cry at that moment? I cannot think of anything that would have made the loss of the election from my point of view more certain.

The whole speech in fact supports the main contention of this book, that the relation between government and opinion is so close that no Government dare act contrary to public opinion. The issue cannot be determined by asserting that public opinion in 1934 and 1935 was wrong. Historians will no doubt argue for centuries whether it was wrong or not. From the historian's point of view, Mr Baldwin's statement of the position was not accurate. The Labour party at Fulham and elsewhere was not "pacifist"; it asserted that even at that late hour (that is, after Sir John Simon's failure to use the League machinery against Japanese aggression) it was possible to maintain peace through the forceful use of the League. That, however, is not the point with which we are concerned. What the speech proves is that the Conservatives were compelled by public opinion in 1935 to undertake to "continue to do all in our power to uphold the Covenant and to maintain and increase the efficiency of the League".

Nevertheless, the example does show the limitations of popular control. It is reasonably certain that in 1935 the people wanted this policy properly carried out. It was supported not only by the main body of the Labour party, but also by a section of middle-class opinion usually described as "the League of Nations Union vote". It is by no means certain that the Government honestly tried to carry out its undertaking. The Labour party would no doubt say that, by following a policy of masterly inactivity, it gradually allowed the situation to worsen so that, when Mr Chamberlain adopted the contrary policy of "appeasement", he probably had a majority for it; and then, when appeasement failed, he had almost unanimous support for a declaration of war. In much the same way, it would be urged, another Chamberlain gradually led the majority of the nation to support a Boer war which, twelve months before, would have been strongly opposed. In other words, though the policy may be determined by public opinion, the execution is in the hands of the Government and, if it is willing to make promises with its tongue in its cheek, it can destroy a policy not by denying it but by undermining it. The only remedy which public opinion possesses is to overthrow the Government at the next opportunity. The Unionist Government which entered into the Boer war went down with a crash in 1906, and the Conservatives might have been out of office for twenty years if there had been no war in 1914. The Chamberlain Government also went out in 1940—and it was clear that the essential cause was the distrust of the "men of Munich".

The example does not demonstrate so clearly that public opinion can be misled. That Mr Baldwin's action cannot be defended constitutionally must be admitted. If he had fully stated the facts, it is possible that, being produced with the authority of the Government, they would have been decisive. The information was given by Mr Churchill, however; and the Labour party did not deny the facts. On the contrary, it admitted the facts but denied the inferences as to policy which Mr Churchill drew from them. It is probably true that the soothing speeches of the National Government prevented the electorate from realising the full implications of the choice before it—large armaments as suggested by Mr Churchill, a strong League of Nations policy as urged by the Labour party, and meek submission and goodwill as suggested by the pacifists led by Mr Lansbury. Some probably thought that there was a fourth possibility, inactivity and blindness as practised by the National Government. It is not true, as Mr Baldwin urged, that "a democracy is always two years behind the dictator". It is true, however, that a democracy like a dictatorship is dependent on the quality of its leaders. The fundamental problem, which no nation has yet solved, is to provide means by which its political leaders can be intelligent and active men.

Finally, there is a seventh point of some importance. The general statement of this chapter assumes that a Government with a majority in the House of Commons can govern subject only to public opinion. With a Conservative Government the assumption is correct.

With any other Government it is not correct because of the permanent Conservative majority in the House of Lords. That majority can be defended if it can be shown that the House of Lords never obstructs a Government except when it is acting contrary to public opinion. Evidence of this kind is not forthcoming; on the contrary, it is easy to produce evidence of the opposite. Nor is it reasonable to expect that any body of men, however able and honest, should be able to act as brokers for a public with the greater part of which they have no contact. The opinions of boards of directors, landowners, St James's clubmen, the Brigade of Guards, and the correspondents of *The Times*, are but minor sections of public opinion. Nor, again, can prominent supporters of the Conservative party be expected to distinguish between the good of the country and the good of their party. Human nature is not made that way. In any case, even if the defence could be proved it would not be complete. A Government's responsibility is to secure acceptance by public opinion not of every proposal, but of its general policy. It can justify itself by works even where it could not produce faith. Public opinion judges the cooking by the pudding, not by the ingredients.

§ 2. *Democracy and Liberty*

With all these qualifications, it is still true that the relation between Government and opinion in Great Britain is very close. It could not be so close but for one factor of which, perhaps, not enough has been said in this book—the general acceptance of the principles of civil liberty. The fact that so little has been said on this subject is in itself evidence of the generality of the acceptance. Civil liberty is so fundamental that a description of it might almost be taken as read. In these days, however, old heresies masquerade under new names and new Huns refine upon the barbarities of the old. To allow the attacks upon the principles of liberty to go by default might be to give the impression not, as is the case, that they are not worthy of being answered, but that they cannot be answered. Nor would it be proper to conclude a survey of the British Constitution without an explanation of the great principles for which the peoples of these islands and of their colonies in North America fought and died.

Emphasis is rightly placed on the laws and institutions which protect liberty in this country. What is less often realised is that liberty is a consequence not of laws and institutions but of an attitude of mind. Laws can be broken and institutions subverted. A people can be forcibly enslaved but it cannot be "forced to be free". It becomes free because it desires to be free, and it remains free because it so intends. Civil and religious liberty came to Great Britain as a lesson drawn from bitter experience. The lesson was first learned in the sphere of religious liberty, though religious and political liberty could not then be clearly distinguished. Those who believe that they have found truth and that those who spurn it have souls in danger of eternal damnation may reasonably think it their duty to stamp out heresy. Roman Catholics, the Reformed Church of England, the Scottish Covenanters, the English "Saints", had their own brands of truth and their own standards of heresy. Oliver Cromwell, the statesman who had to govern a multitude of sects, might make fine speeches on toleration. His secretary, John Milton, might in *Areopagitica* write the finest defence of liberty in the English language. They were, however, in advance of their time. Not until the "age of reason" was it recognised that truth, if there was such a thing, was many-sided and that any Protestant might have learned a portion of it. Not until after Culloden, when Romanism ceased to be sedition,

May Day demonstration

could Roman Catholics begin to live in peace, and not until 1829 were their main legal disabilities swept away. Even the age of reason could not accept agnosticism or atheism as arguable propositions, and the political disabilities of Jews and dissenters were not all abolished until late in the nineteenth century.

In the meantime the connection between religion and politics had become less close. Church patronage was to Walpole a means of keeping the Whigs in power. Bolingbroke could be a Deist (though in private), seek to lead the party of "Church and King", and hold treasonable converse with a Romanist Pretender. A political leader ran the risk of impeachment not because of his religious opinions, but because he had lost his majority. Not until late in the eighteenth century was political opposition pardonable, and even Charles James Fox was struck off the roll of the Privy Council.

It is true that long before the eighteenth century civil liberty in the narrow sense had been established. A host of foreign commentators, such as Montesquieu, Voltaire and de Lolme bore testimony to the freedom that prevailed in England. A conflict against the King and the King's religion was a conflict for the liberty and the property of the individual. The Court of Star Chamber went the way of the Court of High Commission. The abolition of newspaper licensing was almost an accident. The Parliament that tried to exclude James II from the throne passed the Habeas Corpus Act. The Bill of Rights which declared the abdication of James II dealt with jurors and excessive bail. The Act of Settlement which transferred the Crown to a more remote Protestant line provided for the independence of judges. Toleration was being erected into a principle, but it is not too much to say that civil liberty was gradually established as a series of empirical solutions of problems raised by the general and religious opinions of the Stuarts.

The result was, however, clear. The great Whig improvisations became the great Whig principles. All were in danger when the French Revolution sent the old Whigs into the arms of the Tories. Charles James Fox and the second Earl Grey fought a gallant rearguard action, and countless almost unknown heroes resisted in the battle which culminated in the failure of the Six Acts. Earl Grey was carried along on the rising tide of the new middle class, and the Whig principles of 1689 became the principles of both political parties.

To explain what these principles are is no easy matter because their precise connotation varies with the functions of the State. For much of the nineteenth century they meant *laissez-faire*, and they are frequently asserted in that extreme form even to-day, when all parties are more or less collectivist. Even the most concrete application can rarely be stated without qualification. To say that "no man can be kept imprisoned except on the orders of a court", for instance, is false, because lunatics, mental deficients, persons suffering from infectious disease, and so on, may be detained without their consent. It must again be emphasised that liberty is the consequence of an attitude of mind rather than of precise rules. It involves insistence on the idea that the action of the State must be directed to achieve the happiness and prosperity of all sections of the community, without regard to wealth, social prestige, "race" or religion. It recognises that the advantage of the many ought not to be purchased at the expense of the suffering of the few. It stresses the autonomy of the individual without asserting that a substantial degree of regulation may not be desirable. It forbids anti-social activity without making the individual a slave tied to a machine.

These are generalities which give infinite scope for differences of opinion as to their application. If they are applied too widely they tend to the creation of a social and economic anarchy because they make the individual free to be enslaved. If the qualifications are interpreted too widely, they make the individual a slave to a machine. Between the extremes is an area in which true friends of liberty may hold different opinions without denying the essential idea. Within that area British political parties formulate their programmes.

Certain institutions are, however, clearly necessary. The first is an honest and impartial administration of justice. That has certainly been attained. No suggestion of corruption is ever made against our judges. They may often be mistaken; their interpretations may sometimes be warped by the narrow groove in which they have been trained; their remedies may often be unavailable to poor men because they are too costly; but they enjoy a reputation for probity which many nations have cause to envy. Moreover, they are independent of political control and political influence. They take orders from nobody except Parliament and superior courts. Though they cannot rid themselves of political bias and though sometimes they have been appointed (more often in the past than in the past generation) because of their political success, they do their best to be impartial, and they would openly and forcibly spurn any attempt at political pressure.

It is necessary, however, that there should be not only impartiality in the judges but also impartiality in the laws. This does not mean, as some have assumed, that all laws must apply equally to everyone. There must be special laws for bankers, and not everyone is a banker. What it does mean is that the laws must not make irrelevant distinctions. The law of banking must apply equally to all bankers, whether they are Jews or Gentiles, Conservatives or Socialists, Roman Catholics or Quakers, moderate drinkers or total abstainers. The more general the evil to be avoided or the advantage to be gained, the more general the law. The law of murder or of theft can make no distinctions between peers and poets, rich men and poor, public servants and private employees. On the other hand, generality and impartiality do not mean that special classes of persons like publicans or public officials may not have special obligations imposed upon them. Nor does it mean that individual owners may not be deprived of their property or have special restrictions imposed upon it in the general interest. In such a case, one property owner is distinguished from another for relevant and not irrelevant considerations like "race", religion or political opinion. Since there is a differentiation, however, it is recognised that compensation must be paid. In other words, what this application of the general idea means is that deprivation of liberty or property must be by "due process of law". In particular, "race", religion and political opinion are irrelevant except in so far as they tend to promote disorder or subvert our democratic Constitution.

The impartiality of laws is not maintained except by the impartiality of their application. The impartiality of the judges is one means by which this is secured. So far as judges are competent and judicial procedure is appropriate, therefore, the application should be left to the Courts. Frequently, however, judges are incompetent because expert knowledge is required and judicial procedure is inappropriate because its cost and formality hinder proper investigation and prevent poor persons from protecting their interests. Judges cannot administer the law of education; judicial procedure is not an appropriate instrument for determining whether it is reasonable to refuse to allow a house to be built by the side of a main road; the judicial procedure is too dilatory and costly to determine whether John Smith is genuinely in search of work. The greater the activity of the State, therefore, the greater the need for honest and impartial administration. Here, too, the British Constitution teaches more lessons than it can learn. Its success is in part due to the civil service which has already been described; in part it is due to the magnificent system of local government which is, unfortunately, outside the scope of this book. It is, however, also due to the control which the courts exercise over public authorities. This system cannot be praised without qualification, because the methods have been dilatory and expensive, and they have not always been applied with proper understanding of the problems involved. Moreover, the control over central institutions has always been inadequate. The rule that "the King can do no wrong" has sometimes meant that Government Departments can do no wrong. Nevertheless, the courts have set their faces sternly against partiality and corruption, and they have insisted that "justice must not only be done but must be seen to be done".

Of the technical methods by which these functions have been exercised there is no space to write. Every Englishman has heard of *habeas corpus*, because it has sometimes lain near the centre of political controversy. He ought also to know about *mandamus*, prohibition and *certiorari*. Nor is this all. Justice and liberty are not maintained only through remedies with Latin names. It is the ordinary administration of civil and criminal law and the interpretation of administrative statutes which matters most. There are defects with which every lawyer is familiar. There are some methods adopted elsewhere, notably by the French, which might be adopted here. The law is in many parts still the "ungodly jumble" of which Carlyle spoke. Yet this certainly English (and Scottish) law does provide, that no man is penalised because he is a Jew, or poor, or without political or social influence, or because he belongs to a party, or because he has unusual notions about a future life.

Nevertheless, we must return to our main point. All this is not so because of technical devices and peculiar rules of law. The law is what Parliament provides, and it is in Parliament that the focus of our liberties must be found. Civil liberty is a consequence of political liberty, and political liberty is the result of a long evolution. The freedom of debate in Parliament asserted by the Bill of Rights is one of the most important political principles. The symbol of liberty is His Majesty's Opposition. This too requires a background of liberty. Without free elections there can be no true parliamentary freedom— though it was only in 1872 that Parliament was convinced that in order to be free voting must be secret. Without freedom of speech, freedom of public meeting, and freedom of association there cannot be free elections. These liberties are not absolute, for freedom to work the Constitution cannot imply freedom to subvert the Constitution, and there is not always agreement on the extent of the qualifications. Nevertheless, the principles are accepted. Moreover, it is because they are accepted that they remain. A Government with a majority in both Houses would find no technical difficulty in sweeping them away.

It is clear, therefore, that the source of our liberty is not in laws or institutions, but in the spirit of a free people. It is the more firmly founded because it expanded so slowly. The liberty for which our forefathers took up arms was a very limited liberty—freedom for a reformed Church, freedom from royal absolutism, parliamentary freedom. For the rest, liberty has "broadened down from precedent to precedent". The danger now is not from within, but from without. As these words are being written, intolerance, "racial" prejudice, a new persecuting religion which derides all other religions, and an absolutism that decries all moral principles are flying over our heads and dropping their presents from the skies.

§ 3. *Is it a Democracy?*

Some months ago an American citizen wrote to *The Spectator* from Seattle, Washington, to explain why many American citizens were at that time isolationist. His argument included the assertion that Britain was not a democracy in his sense of the term.

> If what you mean by democracy was the system practised in England just before the war, you will find many here in America who will dissent to your use of the term. I, as an American, do not consider equal justice for all as denoting democracy, or even equable political representation. Democracy must stand on a different basis from something which is grudgingly given by a conciliatory upper class to classes which are hard pressing it. Democracy must stand on the ground of the most common and least privileged of the people composing a country. It must first be of the people before it can be by it or for it. Therefore you do not touch us when you say that you are fighting for democracy. You are not fighting for our kind of democracy.

Perhaps the citizen of Seattle now regrets that he wrote this letter. It is idle to dispute about minor differences when great principles are at stake. The statement is nevertheless worth quoting because it represents a point of view that is not to be found only on the shores of Puget Sound. That we have not an egalitarian democracy will be readily agreed; that the United States or the State of Washington has an egalitarian democracy will not be agreed so readily. Comparisons are odious, and few are experienced enough to be able to make them. If it is true, as this book alleges, that there is a close correspondence between the actions of the Government and the opinions of an electorate containing all "the most common and least privileged of the people", it is difficult and, indeed, impossible to assert that this is not a democracy. If it is true, as this Chapter alleges, that British liberty—not merely "equable political representation" and "equal justice for all"—rests on the spirit of a free people, it is difficult to understand how free peoples everywhere can fail to sympathise with it.

The sting of the statement lies, however, in the phrase "grudgingly given by a conciliatory upper class to classes which are hard pressing it". It would be easy to retort with a *tu quoque*. An American citizen in far-off Seattle may be pardoned if he misunderstands who are this "conciliatory upper class". It certainly did not come over with William the Conqueror. It is not the descendants of those who killed each other in the Wars of the Roses. It is not the "new nobility" of the Tudors. It is not the landowners of the eighteenth century, nor even the manufacturers of the nineteenth. At its worst it is no worse than the bankers of Wall Street, the steel kings of Pittsburg, or the lumber kings of Seattle. Vested interests always oppose reforms that seem to threaten them. Our democratic advance has been slow because our people have been conservative. They have recognised that there has been much in established institutions that has been truly admirable, that rapid changes are apt to destroy more than they create, that there is an "inevitability of gradualism" in more senses than one, and that they themselves have much to lose besides their chains. The outpourings of enthusiastic reformers must not be mistaken for the complaints of a frustrated people. If the people of this country want to overthrow capitalism, the public school system, the House of Lords or the monarchy, they have the power in their hands. If they have not done so, the explanation is that they have not wanted to do so. The monarchy, in fact, provides an excellent example. The Americans decided to overthrow monarchy more than 150 years ago. It would be unnecessary now to use the methods that they then used: but there has never been a really serious republican movement—certainly not since Joseph Chamberlain left the Liberal party. The stability of the monarchy does not depend on a condition made by a "conciliatory upper class" in consideration of social reforms. It depends essentially on popular support.

The truth is that "the most common and least privileged of the people" have generally been conservative, while the "conciliatory upper class" has sometimes been, on American standards, quite radical. Thus arises the astonishing homogeneity of our political opinions, to which Bagehot drew attention and which the developments of eighty years have not affected. If it is necessary for democracy that the country should be rent by fierce conflict between the privileged and the under-privileged, we have not a democracy. But that kind of democracy is to be found neither in our books nor in our experience. Democracy, as we understand it, means that the people must be free, the free choose the rulers, and the rulers govern according to the wishes of the people. It is for that kind of democracy that we are fighting.

INDEX

232

INDEX

CAMBRIDGE: PRINTED BY W. LEWIS, M.A., AT THE UNIVERSITY PRESS